NYC
Walks
—
Guide to
New
Architecture

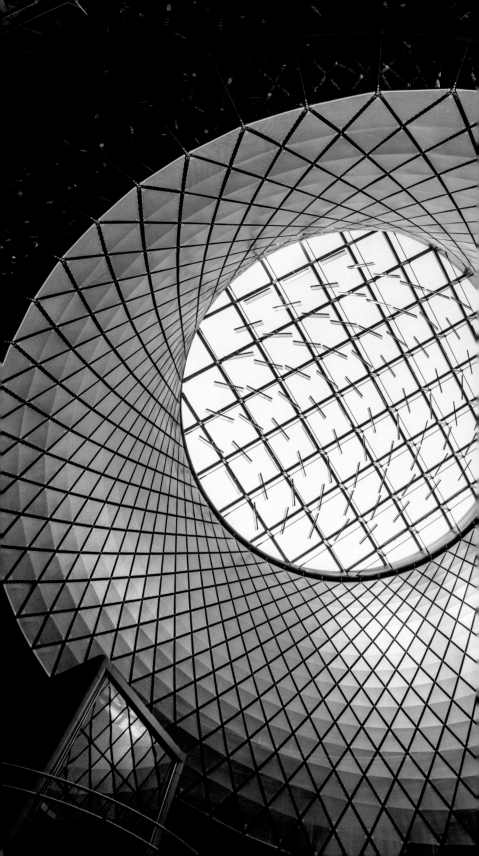

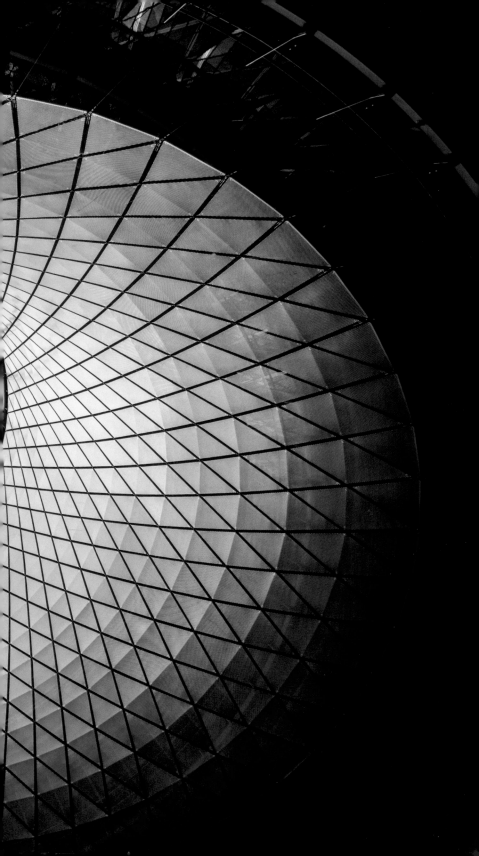

NYC
Walks

—

Guide to
New
Architecture

JOHN HILL

PHOTOGRAPHY BY
PAVEL BENDOV

Prestel
Munich — London — New York

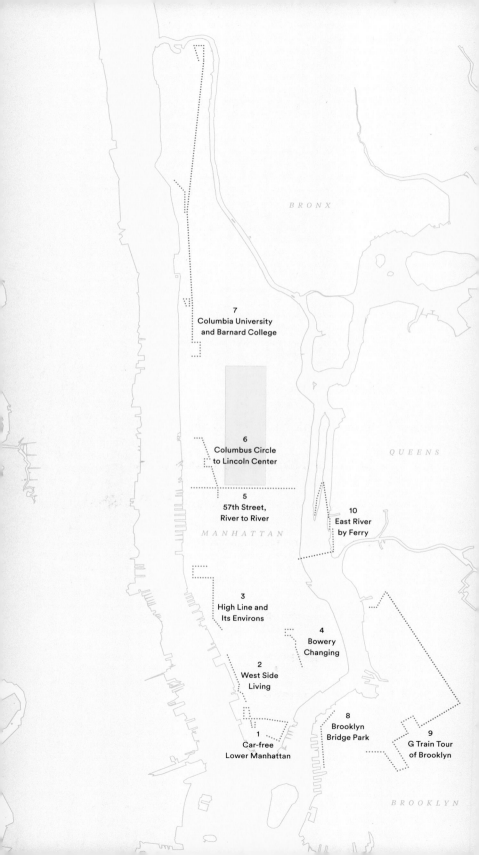

BRONX

7
Columbia University
and Barnard College

6
Columbus Circle
to Lincoln Center

QUEENS

5
57th Street,
River to River

MANHATTAN

10
East River
by Ferry

3
High Line and
Its Environs

4
Bowery
Changing

2
West Side
Living

8
Brooklyn
Bridge Park

9
G Train Tour
of Brooklyn

1
Car-free
Lower Manhattan

BROOKLYN

Contents

Introduction

Welcome to "Paradox NYC"

Walking around New York City leads to the realization that the city is full of contradictions that often find their expression through architecture. A handful of these paradoxical conditions came to the fore after putting into book form the architectural walking tours I've been giving for six years. Described here, they provide a context for the ten tours focused on parts of the city that contain a density of notable new buildings and landscapes.

Building for billionaires
while building affordable housing

Michael Bloomberg, New York City's billionaire mayor from 2002 to 2013, stated just before he left office, "If we could get every billionaire around the world to move here it would be a godsend." Bloomberg saw billionaires as a source of tax revenue that would benefit residents on the lower end of the income totem pole. Unfortunately, condos in the slender towers along Manhattan's 57th Street, aka Billionaires' Row [TOUR 5], have been taxed so far below market value that the property-tax burden has shifted to lower-income renters. To balance condos for the superrich with affordable dwellings, Bloomberg favored an inclusionary housing program and the 421-a tax abatement, both of which encouraged developers to provide affordable units. But the former was voluntary and led to few affordable units, while the latter allowed those units to be built at a distance; the tax breaks at One57, for instance, yielded a few dozen affordable units in the Bronx, miles from 57th Street. Bloomberg's successor, Bill de Blasio, who promised to increase affordable housing, made inclusionary housing mandatory for certain developments, but most of the apartment buildings encountered on these tours were underway before he took office in 2014.

Building for tourists
while building for residents

Just as Bloomberg was luring billionaires through developer incentives, his administration sought to increase the number of tourists visiting the city: more than 54 million came during his last year in office and by 2016 the number topped 60 million. While the city has focused heavily on advertising to promote tourism, architecture has played a role too. The pairing of developers with big-name architects has infused the city with iconic buildings in the vein of Frank Gehry's Guggenheim Museum Bilbao (1997) in Spain. Beyond the now-famous "Bilbao effect," New York City's Department of Design and Construction's Design and Construction Excellence 2.0 program has raised the quality of public buildings across all five boroughs. Yet in regard to high-profile developments, many residents feel left behind. The city-owned High Line [TOUR 3], which draws around eight million people annually, is the most telling example: the elevated park, combined with zoning changes, transformed the area into a playground of luxury housing designed by name-brand architects, ignoring the area's lower-income residents.

Building on the waterfront
while building for resiliency

Long the site of industry, the waterfronts of Manhattan, Brooklyn, and Queens are being transformed into residential neighborhoods and parkland. Massive rezonings have led to residential towers along the East River in Greenpoint and Williamsburg, both in Brooklyn, and Long Island City, Queens [TOUR 10], with prized views of Manhattan. Even before Hurricane Sandy hit in October 2012, though, the building of waterfront developments was myopic, antithetical to the rising sea levels that will accompany climate change. The preferred means of addressing storm surges and rising waters at these and other spots of new waterfront construction have been landscapes: parks as buffers between water and buildings. Landscape architects have responded with designs that provide social and recreational amenities, as in Brooklyn Bridge Park [TOUR 8].

Building for security
while building for freedom

The events of September 11, 2001, have impacted the security of buildings and cities well outside of New York City. Here, 9/11 led to the closures of previously accessible spaces, such as the lobbies of office buildings, and reshaped the city's streetscapes as rows of bollards. Yet coinciding with these and other protective measures was the co-option of car space for pedestrians, spearheaded by Mayor Bloomberg's transportation commissioner Janette Sadik-Khan, most visibly in the closing of Broadway in Times Square. The two approaches—increased security and the creation of pedestrian zones—converge at the 16-acre (6.4 ha) World Trade Center site [TOUR 1], where formerly de-mapped streets would be knitted back into the fabric of Lower Manhattan. At least that was the idea: in actuality, the New York City Police Department (NYPD) eventually fortified the site's perimeter and closed the streets to traffic.

"Building like Moses with Jacobs in mind"

These words, spoken by former NYC Planning Commissioner Amanda Burden, sum up the Bloomberg administration's reshaping of the city. Put simply, New York 'master builder' Robert Moses was known for getting projects—many of them big, such as Lincoln Center [TOUR 6]—done, while author and urban activist Jane Jacobs embraced the diversity and small details of urban life. Theirs were two poles that never met, until Bloomberg helped jump-start a number of large developments—Pacific Park [TOUR 9], Hudson Yards [TOUR 3], and Columbia University in Manhattanville [TOUR 7] among them—all the while creating pocket plazas, improving bike lanes, embracing projects like the High Line, and generally making the public realm safer and more enjoyable. With developments like Hudson Yards unfolding over decades, the imprint of the Bloomberg administration continues, as the tours in this book make readily apparent.

Some Practical Notes

NYC Walks: Guide to New Architecture collects eight architectural walking tours I've been giving since the publication of my first book, *Guide to Contemporary New York City Architecture*, in late 2011, adding two specially made tours for an even ten. Accompanying my descriptions and directions are maps and photos that should, respectively, make the routes easy to follow and the book great to look at, even at a distance from NYC.

This book's title implies that walking is the best means of seeing the city's constantly changing built environment, but it also means, inadvertently, that the routes are not fully accessible, since most involve stairs, better known as impediments to anyone with a mobility disability. Similarly, access to buildings is limited and should be gained only when indicated in the text. To ensure access, it's recommended that the tours be tackled during the day rather than at night, and on weekdays or Saturdays rather than on Sundays or holidays.

For reasons of space and with just a few exceptions, attribution is limited to the primary architects over the full team of consultants necessary for any architectural project. Clients are indicated when known, while names of the roughly 150 projects are either official, given by the architect, or, lacking those, their address, which are provided for all projects when known.

Tours are numbered while the buildings and landscapes are lettered, resulting in a designation system (One57 is 5F, for instance) that allows cross-referencing across chapters.

Lastly, even though the focus of this book is new architecture, it dos not ignore important historical buildings and landscapes along the routes; these, as well as some notable projects underway at the time of writing, are underlined in the text.

1 Car-free Lower Manhattan

3.75 MILES / 6 KM

> *This tour starts at the intersection of Wall Street and Broadway and ends at the World Trade Center.*

Our first tour confronts New York City's early history more than any other tour presented here; after all, the city was born in Lower Manhattan. We start on Wall Street, the northern defensive boundary of the Dutch New Amsterdam and the heart of the Financial District; traipse through a couple of historic districts; wend our way from the East River waterfront to the Battery Park City waterfront; and end, suitably, at the most high-profile and contested development site in the city. At nearly four miles (6.4 km), the route is long (if necessary, it can be easily split into two: A–F and G–S) but also an unconventional one, traversing many of the area's pedestrian-only thoroughfares: the streets that have been closed to traffic for security and entertainment; the waterfront promenades that followed the closing of the city's ports; the Privately Owned Public Spaces (POPS) that developers created to gain extra square footage in their towers; and the enclosed concourses tunneling under and bridging over the city streets. While not entirely car free, by focusing on pedestrian routes this tour looks at the public realm *between* the buildings as much as the buildings themselves.

Walk east on Wall Street past the New York Stock Exchange (NYSE) to the security bollards outside 40 Wall Street.

A NYSE Financial District Streetscapes & Security

ROGERS MARVEL ARCHITECTS, 2004 – WALL STREET AND BROAD STREET

Immediately after the 9/11 attacks, lines of garbage trucks blocked the intersections leading to the NYSE. Three years later, a more permanent—and pleasing—solution finally displaced them: faceted bronze bollards and pivoting "turntables" that allow authorized vehicles to pass. Although the design by the firm of Rob Rogers and Jonathan Marvel (both of whom have since formed their own eponymous offices) is contemporary,

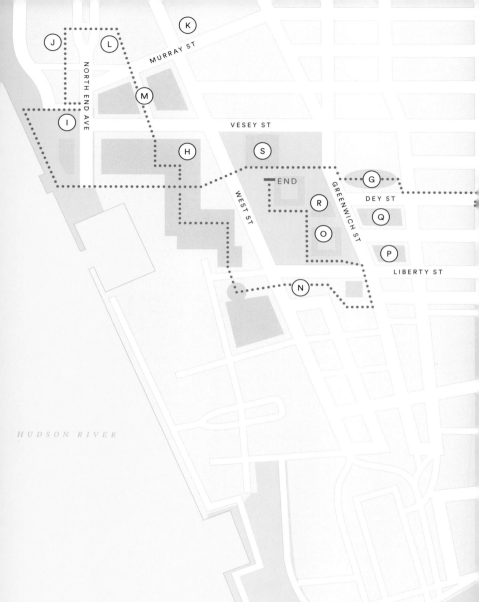

MURRAY ST

NORTH END AVE

VESEY ST

WEST ST

GREENWICH ST

DEY ST

LIBERTY ST

END

HUDSON RIVER

J · L · K · M · I · H · S · G · R · Q · O · P · N

F Fulton Center

NASSAU ST
WILLIAM ST
FULTON ST
JOHN ST
FRONT ST
E Pier 17
D1 Pier 15
D East River Waterfront Esplanade
START
A NYSE Financial District
WALL ST
EAST RIVER
GOUVERNEUR LN
C Pier 11, Wall Street Ferry Terminal
STONE ST
PEARL ST
WATER ST
B The Elevated Acre

A   NYSE Financial District
    Streetscapes & Security
B   The Elevated Acre
C   Pier 11, Wall Street Ferry Terminal
D   East River Waterfront Esplanade
D1 Pier 15
E   Pier 17
F   Fulton Center
G   World Trade Center
    Transportation Hub
H   Pavilion at Brookfield Place
I   Irish Hunger Memorial
J   Teardrop Park South
K   111 Murray Street
L   Asphalt Green Battery Park City
M   Arcade Canopy
N   Liberty Park
O   National September 11 Memorial
P   4 World Trade Center
Q   3 World Trade Center
R   National September 11
    Memorial Museum
S   One World Trade Center

approval had to be obtained from the New York City Landmarks Preservation Commission (LPC) since the structures overlap with the historic street plan of New Amsterdam and Colonial New York, designated in 1983. Recently, the cobbled streets around the NYSE have become littered with fences, checkpoints, and other ad hoc barriers—ugly counterpoints to the bespoke, tasteful bronze bollards that serve as points of entry to the city's center of finance.

Walk east on Wall Street to Hanover Street, then right three short blocks down to Hanover Square.

Dedicated in 2012 as The Queen Elizabeth II September 11th Garden, this small triangular public space dates back to the 1700s and British rule. Landscape designers Julian and Isabel Bannerman added sinuous sandstone benches meant to echo the shape of the British Isles, though the undulating lines also remind us that the space used to sit at the water's edge, before landfill widened the tip of the island.

Cross the street south of Hanover Square to Stone Street.

The Stone Street Historic District consists of about a dozen storehouses built just after the Great Fire of 1835 on a street the *New York Times* described as "a dingy, ill-kept back alley" just before it was designated by LPC in 1996. New stone paving improved conditions, but it wasn't until the street was closed to cars and filled with tables and chairs in 2003 that this short street became a popular spot for workday lunches.

Continue south to the end of Stone Street, turn left and head east on Coenties Slip across Pearl Street. At Water Street turn left, walk north along the arcade, and take the escalators or stairs on the right.

(B) The Elevated Acre
ROGERS MARVEL ARCHITECTS & KEN SMITH WORKSHOP, 2005 –
55 WATER STREET

The pleasing character of the aptly named Elevated Acre is far removed from its original incarnation when 55 Water Street was built in 1970, two years after the city allowed raised plazas as POPS. There were hopes the plaza would connect to the riverfront by bridging FDR Drive, but that never materialized, and the hardscape plaza was little used. In 2001 Goldman Sachs considered building its headquarters in place of the plaza and the parking garage beneath it, but when the company opted to build elsewhere the owner of 55 Water decided to renovate the POPS. Subsequently, architects Rob Rogers and Jonathan Marvel

(B)

and landscape architect Ken Smith won a design competition for the one-acre (0.4 ha) space.

The reworked escalators and stairs between 55 Water's tall tower on the south and shorter mass on the west deliver you up to a landscape of "dunes" separated by intimate pockets with seating. A lawn of artificial turf seems to connect to the upper floors of the former New York City Police Museum across the street; combined with concrete steps, the lawn doubles as a venue for outdoor movies. Benches at the far, eastern edge of the Elevated Acre are set up for views of Brooklyn and its namesake bridge. Punctuating the raised plaza is a glass lantern (a collaboration with lighting designer Jim Conti) that cycles through different colors after sundown. The plaza is popular for workday lunches, though the sounds from FDR Drive and the heliport at Pier 6 keep it from being *too* popular.

Exit the Elevated Acre back to Water Street, turn right and walk north past Old Slip Park until you reach the narrow Gouverneur Lane; turn right and head east until you walk under FDR Drive.

(C) Pier 11, Wall Street Ferry Terminal
SMITH-MILLER + HAWKINSON ARCHITECTS, 2000

To fix up an old pier one block south of Wall Street and better serve the water taxis and ferries docking there, the city undertook improvements (by landscape architect Judith Heintz) and added an enclosed waiting area with restrooms and a kiosk totaling around 200 square feet (18.6 sq m). Designed by Henry

Smith-Miller and Laurie Hawkinson, the enclosed metal-and-glass box literally opens up in decent weather: a large south-facing glass wall lifts below an exposed steel beam to shade people waiting for a ferry. Some restoration remedied damage from Hurricane Sandy, but the small building now sits on a pier crowded with a Citi Bike station, a large gate and enclosures at the foot of the pier, and, most unfortunately, a canopy impeding the southern view from the waiting room.

Walk north up the esplanade via the steel grating over the water and stop at the waterfront steps aligned with Wall Street.

From here, the metal wall on the north side of Pier 11 is visible, its name emblazoned in yellow graphics that wrap over the angled roof to be visible from helicopters overhead.

Continue north up the esplanade to the benches opposite the restaurant pavilion tucked below FDR Drive.

(D) East River Waterfront Esplanade

SHOP ARCHITECTS & KEN SMITH WORKSHOP, 2011

A Guggenheim Museum designed by Frank Gehry was planned for this spot but shelved in 2002. Two years later the city initiated a plan to transform a two-mile (3.2 km) stretch of the formerly industrial waterfront—from the Battery Maritime Building at the tip of the island to East River Park north of the Manhattan Bridge—into a green space with an esplanade, bike lanes, seating, dog runs, pavilions, and other amenities. The first phase of the four-phase East River Waterfront Esplanade, stretching from Wall Street to Maiden Lane, opened to the public in summer 2011.

The biggest hurdle in both getting to the waterfront and transforming it into a popular recreational strip was the South Street Viaduct, which was built in 1954 to connect FDR Drive with the Battery Park Underpass and complete a peripheral system of Manhattan expressways. The design team overcame this condition by placing certain amenities (dog run, restaurant, restrooms) beneath the elevated road and selectively painting and illuminating the overhead structure (a purple beam on the east side stands out the most). Besides the standard bike lane, the design consists of large hexagonal pavers in various colors, planters with native trees and plants, and plenty of wood benches. Some unique features include steps leading down to the water, such as those aligned with Wall Street, bar seating for eating lunch along the railings, and the aforementioned pavilions; one of them, the restaurant next to us, has a perforated metal enclosure, glass walls, and a generous overhang that entice people to actually hang out beneath an overpass.

 ## Pier 15

SHOP ARCHITECTS & KEN SMITH WORKSHOP, 2011

The design parti of Pier 15 is evident from this spot: two glass boxes, one at either end, holding up a cantilevered roof-deck. The glass enclosure on the west has information and ticket booths for cruises launching from the pier, while the one at the far end houses a bar.

Walk up the esplanade to the foot of Pier 15.

There are a couple of alternatives for tackling the pier: walk up to the roof-deck (via the stairs on the right or the ramp on the left) or walk out at the level of the esplanade. Opt for the latter to experience the pier's best detail: the bright red slats of the ceiling that weave into a hull-like form. At the tip of the pier is an open expanse with benches and steps that descend toward the water. From here you can head up via the stairs on the north side of the pier and stand at the ship-like prow of the top deck. After that, walk across the roofscape, letting the spectacular views return you back to the esplanade.

Walk up the esplanade past the "Street of Ships" docked at Pier 16.

Pier 17

SHOP ARCHITECTS, 2018

This four-story glass box replaces the previous Pier 17, a three-story structure that looked old but dated back to only 1985.

Designed by Benjamin Thompson, it had functioned as a shopping mall with two indoor atria and outdoor balconies. Pier 17 was the last element in the Rouse Company's transformation of the South Street Seaport—designated a landmark district in 1977—into a festival market similar to the developer's Quincy Market in Boston. Commercial success of the mall and the larger Seaport area ebbed and flowed over the years, but in 2010, Texas-based developer Howard Hughes Corporation took over the lease of the city-owned Seaport and subsequently spent nearly three-quarters of a billion dollars retooling the area for inhabitants (millennials, mainly) rather than tourists, rebranding it the Seaport District. With the demolition of Pier 17, away went the chains found in every suburban mall, and with new construction, in came restaurants by celebrity chefs, a studio for ESPN, and a huge 1.5-acre (0.6 ha) rooftop.

The lower two floors of Pier 17 cater to small shops and restaurants, laid out by SHoP Architects like a modern village of metal-and-wood-clad volumes. Portions of the base are enclosed in retractable glass walls that stay open in warm weather and open up views toward the Brooklyn Bridge, best seen from the eastern end of the pier. The façades on the upper two floors where larger floor plates serve commercial tenants are wrapped in an alternating rhythm of translucent channel glass and tall windows. Exposed steel framing extends past the channel glass to hint at the rooftop park. Designed with James Corner Field Operations, who also handled the promenades around and beneath the building, the rooftop is anchored by a 60,000-square-foot (5,574 sq m) open-air performance space. Accompanying it would be a planned seasonal art piece (more "architecture" than "art"): a lightweight canopy designed by German architect Achim Menges and woven by robots with noncorrosive materials ideally suited for its waterfront location.

After exploring Pier 17, head back to the esplanade at Fulton Street.

One element not completed as of this writing is the renovation of the early twentieth-century Tin Building, once part of the Fulton Fish Market. Vacant since 2006 after the market relocated to less-prime real estate in the Bronx, the three-story building was damaged during Hurricane Sandy in 2012, and as part of Howard Hughes Corporation's development, was lifted above the 100-year floodplain.

Cross South Street and walk west on Fulton Street to Front Street, noting the view up ahead of Frank Gehry's residential tower (2011) at 8 Spruce Street.

Dominating this intersection—the convergence of the Seaport District's Belgian block–paved, pedestrian-only streets—are the rhythmic chimneys of Schermerhorn Row, the most remarkable collection of nineteenth-century commercial buildings in the area, if not the whole city. Their preservation (and that of the larger area) stems from the efforts of the South Street Seaport Museum, which was founded in 1967 and has its main venue at 12 Fulton Street in the middle of the Row. These and other 1800s buildings east of Pearl Street were built on low-lying landfill, one reason the waters from Sandy reached as much as eight feet (2.4 m) deep here.

Turn left and walk south on Front Street until John Street.

The footprint of the nautically themed Imagination Playground resembles a ship that would have docked in Burling Slip two centuries ago. This playground is the first permanent version of Imagination Playground, an idea developed by architect David Rockwell where creative, free play is paramount; its most recognizable component is the blue foam blocks that litter the playground's midsection.

Turn right and walk west along the south side of John Street to Gold Street.

Once known as the insurance district, most of the buildings along this part of the walk have since been converted to residences, minus a couple of POPS highlighted here.

A few steps past Gold Street is an atrium walkway from 1972 that cuts diagonally beneath 100 William Street, brightened with a new lobby and illuminated pillars by Rogers Marvel Architects in this century.

After walking through the atrium, cross William Street
and walk along the plaza facing the impressive Federal
Reserve Bank of New York (1924) to 33 Maiden Lane at
the corner.

This postmodern office tower (1986) by Philip Johnson and
John Burgee features rounded brick piers and a barrel-vaulted
pedestrian space that connects to the subway. But the building
is more interesting for what it's not: a daring proposal from the
early 1970s by architect Kevin Roche for the Federal Reserve Bank
of New York—an unbuilt tower that would have been lifted on
four large columns thirteen stories above a ground-level plaza.
Although the bank bought space in a nearby building instead, it
ironically bought the Johnson/Burgee building in 2016.

Walk through the pedestrian space to Nassau Street,
head north and at John Street, turn left and continue
to the west side of Broadway.

(F) Fulton Center

ARUP & GRIMSHAW ARCHITECTS, 2014 – 200 BROADWAY

At a cost of $1.4 billion, the new Fulton Center was far from cheap,
though as we'll see it's not nearly the most expensive transit
project in Lower Manhattan. Funded primarily through post-9/11
federal recovery funds, the project is visible as a three-story glass
box with a conical dome rising above it, but it also consists of
new underground passages serving ten subway lines, new street
entrances (such as the one behind us), the rehabilitation of four
existing subway stations, and the restoration of the slender Corbin
Building designed by Francis H. Kimball from 1888–9, visible on
the northeast corner of John Street and Broadway. A nine-story
interstitial structure, covered partly in fritted glass, sits between
the landmark building and the main body of the new Fulton
Center, which is articulated as a glass curtain wall set behind a
dark steel structure.

Cross Broadway and enter Fulton Center.
Take the stairs down one level and stop at the
opening in the center of the atrium.

The raison d'être of the dome glimpsed from outside is in full
bloom here. Called *Sky Reflector-Net*, the metal lining designed
by James Carpenter Design Associates with Schlaich Bergermann
Partner hangs from above by a cable net. Created as part of
the Metropolitan Transit Authority (MTA) Arts & Design percent
for art program, the architectural artwork brings daylight down
to the below-grade floors of the Fulton Center via 952 aluminum

reflectors and the skylight's angular slant toward the southeast. *Sky Reflector-Net* serves a secondary purpose: it partially shields the retail and commercial spaces that wrap the atrium behind angled, relatively ordinary glass walls.

> *Head up the escalator to the northeast; turn right and walk*
> *around the atrium toward John Street; then take the escalator*
> *down to the Dey Street Concourse.*

The escalator cutting through the brick foundations of the Corbin Building is an unexpected and memorable experience— a historic, subterranean flip side to the soaring metallic artwork over the atrium. While the same can't be said about the block-long Dey Street Concourse, whose most memorable feature is the crisscrossing lights overhead, it is for us a relevant car-free way of accessing the World Trade Center (WTC) site.

(G) World Trade Center Transportation Hub

SANTIAGO CALATRAVA, 2016 – 185 GREENWICH STREET

The fairly standard glass doors at the end of the concourse provide an un-ceremonial entrance to the soaring space beyond: the Oculus, the heart of Santiago Calatrava's $4 billion WTC Transportation Hub. Of course, after descending a few steps to the marble floor that sits 16 stories beneath the 330-foot-long (100 m) skylight, the first question might be, "Where are the trains?" Although the unmistakably "Calatrava" creation of parallel steel ribs was unveiled in 2004 as a replacement for both the PATH (Port Authority Trans-Hudson) station destroyed on 9/11 and

its temporary replacement built in 2003, the reality that arrived a dozen years later is that the Spanish architect/engineer basically designed a mall—Westfield World Trade Center, to be precise. Two floors of high-end stores line both sides of the elliptical space, with even more shops extending from the space along the concourses to 4 World Trade Center and One World Trade Center.

The Port Authority transit agency wanted to create "a Grand Central Terminal in Lower Manhattan," but aside from the immensity of their main halls, they are much different beasts. Grand Central, with its un-mall-like space, handles 750,000 riders every weekday, while the PATH's ridership between New York and New Jersey is only 60,000 every weekday. The Hub's mall bulks up its daily population and justifies the Oculus's existence.

The skeletal steel ribs of the Oculus—as common a feature in Calatrava's buildings as their escalating costs—culminate in an operable skylight that opens every September 11. The ribs, as we'll see later, extend outward to give the building its distinctive birdlike form. From inside, though, it's difficult to see these "wings" through the dense array of ribs, the number of which were doubled up per the demands of the New York City Police Department (NYPD).

Walk to the west end of the Oculus and down the steps to near the PATH turnstiles.

Calatrava's skeletal structure reaches outward from the footprint of the Oculus, most strikingly with the undulating beams over the mezzanine to the PATH platforms one level down. Resembling the rib cage of an alien creature, the row of beams changes slightly from one to the next, arching downward until the beam at the far end nearly touches the marble floor.

⋮ *Head right toward the West Concourse.*

In 2013, three years before the Hub's official opening, the West Concourse opened, connecting the interim PATH terminal with Battery Park City. Retail storefronts line the north side of the concourse on two levels, while opposite is a solid wall with a long digital billboard. Why not shops on both sides? On the other side of the marble wall is the footprint of the National September 11 Memorial's north pool.

⋮ *Walk to the west end of the concourse and ascend*
⋮ *the escalator.*

(H) Pavilion at Brookfield Place
PELLI CLARKE PELLI ARCHITECTS, 2013 – 230 VESEY STREET

The architects have described this entry pavilion facing the six-lane West Street as "the new front door into Brookfield Place," the retail and office complex formerly known as the World Financial Center. Curving glass walls with glass fins provide generous views of One World Trade Center and the rest of the WTC site across the street, but it's the two treelike, 54-foot-tall (16.4 m) columns that attract the most attention. Not merely an architectural statement, the diagrid structure responds to site restrictions (the concourse and PATH tunnel left only two spots for columns) and the need for the two columns to support the roof *and* glass curtain wall. The six-inch (15 cm) steel tubes are woven in two layers, tied together with tension/compression rings. Inadvertently, these woven-steel "trees" ready us for the palm trees in the Winter Garden beyond.

Walk west out of the pavilion, around the shops, and into the Winter Garden.

Three decades before Cesar Pelli's firm gave Brookfield Place their "new front door," he designed the World Financial Center, an 8.9-million-square-foot (827,000 sq m), four-tower commercial development in Battery Park City. At its heart was the glass-roofed Winter Garden, a grand space that was damaged on 9/11; Brookfield Properties, which had operated the complex since 1996, promptly rebuilt the large space and reopened it in 2002. The 120-foot-tall (36.6 m) space is still punctuated by a grove of sixteen palm trees from California but now accompanied by an adjacent market and food hall.

Exit the Winter Garden to the waterside plaza and continue west to the waterfront belvedere.

Battery Park City (BPC) occupies 92 acres (37 ha) of landfill created by the excavation of the World Trade Center. The plan for a mixed-use neighborhood on the site of twenty industrial piers in the Hudson River was hatched politically in 1966 and envisioned a few years later as superblocks—a floating patch of Modernism disconnected from the dense, historic Financial District. But following the fiscal crisis of the subsequent decade, Battery Park City Authority (BPCA) shifted to a contextual master plan that extended the existing streets westward to knit the landfill development with downtown Manhattan. The master plan developed by Alexander Cooper and Stanton Eckstut in 1979 was carried out over the next three decades, with only one component of the original Modernist plan realized: Gateway Plaza, the gray towers visible across the yacht harbor. Pelli's commercial core was built in 1989, while the south residential neighborhood filled in soon after and the north residential neighborhood that we'll traverse came largely after the turn of the millennium.

Key to BPC's success is not the buildings—conservative brick-and-stone edifices—but the public spaces that take up thirty percent of its acreage. They consist of parks and public art sprinkled throughout BPC and, most successfully, a riverfront esplanade running 1.2 miles (1.9 km) from the southern tip at Battery Park to one block north of Chambers Street. Designed by Alexander Cooper and landscape architect Laurie Olin, the esplanade is basically a wide sidewalk with hexagonal asphalt pavers, benches, and plantings that connects its parks, namely Robert F. Wagner Jr. Park, South Cove Park, and Rockefeller Park. Here, just north of the cove, is one of BPC's most recognizable artworks: Martin Puryear's *Pylons*.

*Walk north on the BPC esplanade past the Port Authority
ferry terminal on the Hudson River and take a soft right.*

(I) Irish Hunger Memorial

1100 ARCHITECT, BRIAN TOLLE & GAIL WITTWER-LAIRD, 2002 –
VESEY STREET AND NORTH END AVENUE

Following a trip that the BPCA president and New York State
governor made to Ireland in 1999, a competition was held
to create a memorial to the country's mid-nineteenth-century
famine. Located on a traffic circle at the end of Vesey Street,
the winning design—by artist Brian Tolle with architects David
Piscuskas and Juergen Riehm of 1100, and landscape architect
Gail Wittwer-Laird—lifts up a quarter-acre (0.1 ha) landscape
of plants indigenous to County Mayo, accompanied by a
reconstructed cottage from the area. Access is via a portal
beneath the 25-foot (7.6 m) cantilever in concrete that works
with the walls—alternating bands of Kilkenny limestone
and backlit glass—to be a contemporary counterpoint to the
transplanted vernacular above.

*After walking through the memorial, head north
across River Terrace through the portal in the Riverhouse
condominiums facing the street.*

(J) Teardrop Park South

MICHAEL VAN VALKENBURGH ASSOCIATES, 2006/2010

Some of the most creative and diverse landscape designs at BPC
are also the most secluded. The 1.8-acre (0.7 ha) Teardrop Park
and the smaller Teardrop Park South sit on two blocks between

(J)

35

five residential towers. There is a strong interdependency between the park and three of the five towers: Teardrop Park is irrigated from the treated gray water of the Solaire (Pelli Clarke Pelli, 2002); the U-shaped Riverhouse (Ennead Architects, 2009) keeps sunlight from reaching Teardrop Park South; to overcome that issue a trio of computer-operated heliostats atop the Verdesian (Pelli Clarke Pelli, 2006) reflect sunlight onto the plants and people using the space.

⋮ *Cross Murray Street and walk north into the middle of*
⋮ *Teardrop Park.*

The long slide in Teardrop Park hints at its dramatic topography, but it hardly prepares you for the impressive Ice Wall, named for the stunning ice formations sometimes visible on the jagged bluestone surface. Most striking is the way the stones are stacked on the 27-foot-tall (8.2 m), 168-foot-long (51 m) wall, as if the rock below Manhattan is breaking through BPC's landfill.

⋮ *Walk east out of Teardrop Park, cross North End Avenue, and*
⋮ *then stop at the raised plaza overlooking the BPC Ball Fields.*

(K) 111 Murray Street

KPF, 2018

Although not the tallest tower in Tribeca (56 Leonard [2A] takes that honor), the 59-story tower due east across the ball fields and West Street appears taller than its 792 feet (241 m). This stems from its slenderness, the curved corners of the glass curtain wall, the gentle outward flare that starts at the 40th floor, and the asymmetrical slant of its glass crown. Designed by KPF for Fisher Brothers and Witkoff, the tower provides 157 residences on land formerly occupied by St. John's University (the school moved to 51 Astor Place [4Q]).

(L) Asphalt Green Battery Park City

HANRAHAN MEYERS ARCHITECTS, 2013 – 212 NORTH END AVENUE

The plaza we are standing on is actually the roof of a fitness and community center that forms the base of the last two residential towers in BPC: Liberty Green and Liberty Luxe (both Ehrenkrantz Eckstut & Kuhn, 2011). Designed by Thomas Hanrahan and

(L)

Victoria Meyers (who also worked on the master plan for the north residential neighborhood), the two-story building provides a gymnasium, pools, fitness center, auditorium, classrooms, and other facilities. At street level, the center run by Asphalt Green provides a block-long plaza on the east side of the towers, with benches overlooking the AstroTurf fields as well as the towers of Lower Manhattan beyond. At the lower level, the building is defined by a 550-foot-long (167.6 m) curved wall of glass, opened up in a few places for small courtyards that provide access to the building and to the plaza above.

Walk down the stairs to the level of the ball fields, turn right and head south along the curved wall then cross Murray Street.

(M) Arcade Canopy

PRESTON SCOTT COHEN, 2010 – NORTH END WAY

The only two commercial buildings in BPC outside of Brookfield Place are the two buildings sitting on this block to the north of it. Between the Conrad Hotel and Goldman Sachs headquarters (Pei Cobb Freed & Partners, 2010) is this narrow pedestrian arcade lined with shops and restaurants. Goldman Sachs owns the whole block, and it hired architect Preston Scott Cohen to cap the 11,000-square-foot (1,021 sq m) walkway with a glass canopy. He responded with folded planes of glass that invite people into the space, shelter them from the elements, and create a pedestrian scale for the tight gap.

Coming through the arcade, cross Vesey Street into Brookfield Place, then take the stairs to the second floor and follow the mall to the Winter Garden and the top of its circular stairs.

This spot, part of a second-floor concourse linking the four towers of Brookfield Place, affords a view through the Pavilion [H] to the World Trade Center site, the final destination on this tour.

Walk south and follow the meandering concourse to the enclosed bridge across Liberty Street, continue left across the enclosed bridge over West Street to the WTC site.

What to build on the site of the 16-acre (6.5 ha) World Trade Center complex was a contentious process, with some figures calling for rebuilding Minoru Yamasaki's Twin Towers after they fell on 9/11. Two of nine entries in the 2002–3 competition for the master plan of the WTC site featured pairs of towers; the entry by the THINK team was a favorite of the Lower Manhattan Development Corporation (LMDC). But in February 2003,

Governor George Pataki stepped in and selected Studio Daniel Libeskind's "Memory Foundations," which placed five glass towers around a below-grade memorial that preserved the footprints of the Twin Towers. The tops of the towers sloped toward the memorial to accentuate the importance of memory over money, while the towers grew in height in a counterclockwise arrangement, culminating in the Freedom Tower and its symbolic height of 1,776 feet (541 m). Though many of the details in his plan changed over time, most of the main ingredients remain: office towers surrounding the memorial, streets reintroduced into and across the site, and construction of New York City's tallest building.

(N) Liberty Park

AECOM, 2016 – 155 CEDAR STREET

Under the guise of the master plan and the site's stringent security measures, the WTC Vehicular Security Center and Tour Bus Parking Facility (VSC), a large underground network of garages and roadways, was created. Its entrance is also the structure that supports the park we're standing on. Landscape architect Joseph E. Brown designed the 1-acre (0.4 ha) park with angular, tapered concrete planters, brick-paved walkways, and wood benches, some built into the edges of the planters. The park features three special elements: Fritz Koenig's *Sphere*, which sat on the original WTC plaza and was recovered from the rubble of the 9/11 attacks; Douwe Blumberg's America's Response Monument, a figural statue completed in 2011; and the new home of the St. Nicholas Greek Orthodox Church and National Shrine, designed by Santiago Calatrava. Originally located at grade roughly where Blumberg's statue is located, Calatrava designed the new St. Nicholas (on hold at the time of writing) as a luminous domed structure at the east end of the park.

Walk to the east end of the park around the rear of St. Nicholas, descend the ramp, then cross Liberty Street and stop at the corner of the memorial plaza.

Gracing the 25-foot-tall (7.6 m) VSC wall facing the memorial is a 336-foot-long (102 m) vertical garden with twenty thousand evergreen ground covers and flowering perennials housed in more than eight hundred rectangular panels. The green wall and its various hues soften an otherwise ugly, utilitarian elevation. Also evident at this intersection is how security restrictions have impacted the WTC site at street level, with bollards ringing the plaza and every other element at WTC, and Greenwich Street and others being closed to traffic.

Walk to the edge of the 9/11 Memorial's south pool.

(O) National September 11 Memorial

MICHAEL ARAD AND PETER WALKER, 2011 – 180 GREENWICH STREET

The LMDC ran the 2003–4 Memorial Competition as an open international competition with thirteen jurors. One of them, Maya Lin, who changed the course of memorials with her Vietnam Veterans Memorial in Washington, DC, was a strong advocate of the winner, architect Michael Arad's *Reflecting Absence*. His vision of an empty plaza with water cascading into voids in the footprints of the Twin Towers certainly recalls the pared-down nature of Lin's memorial in DC, but after Arad's design was selected as a finalist

from the 5,200 other entries, landscape architect Peter Walker joined the architect to add a grove of trees, softening some of *Reflecting Absence*'s harder edges. More changes came after the jury officially selected the Arad/Walker scheme in January 2004. Most significantly, the names of the victims of the 2001 attacks and 1993 bombing were moved from below-grade galleries— adjacent to the footprints and behind sheets of water falling from above—to plaza level, where they were cut into bronze railings overlooking the pools. Yet even with the changes wrought by money and politics, the memorial is a remarkable achievement— if a pricey one at more than a half-billion dollars.

The plaza is basically a grove of more than four hundred swamp white oaks surrounding the pools, set into parallel east-west rows between granite paving and seating. Constructed as a green roof over the VSC, the PATH station and tracks, the 9/11 Museum [R], and other below-grade elements, the trees sit in 40,000 tons (36,278 tonnes) of soil, while drains in the plaza collect rainwater to irrigate the grove. Similar technical feats were required for Arad's granite-lined pools, which circulate around 50,000 gallons (227 kl) of water every minute. The pumped water appears first in a trough below the bronze railings, travels over a rounded weir, then falls 30 feet (9 m) in a din loud enough to drown out the city's noises. Finally, the water falls into a smaller opening in the center of each footprint—a void within the void—what is literally and figuratively the deepest aspect of the memorial.

> *Walk to the western edge of the south pool for views of 3WTC*
> *and 4WTC.*

4 World Trade Center

MAKI AND ASSOCIATES, 2013 – 150 GREENWICH STREET

Fumihiko Maki's 4WTC, to the right, was the first tower completed on the WTC site (7WTC, designed by SOM, was completed in 2006 one block north). Designed for developer Larry Silverstein, who famously signed a lease for the Twin Towers in July 2001, the tower opened in November 2013. The 72-story tower rises to 977 feet (298 m) in three plan-shapes: a three-story trapezoidal base that fills the site; a parallelogram up to floor 54; and a smaller trapezoid at the upper floors. The western face at the top of the tower looks toward the memorial, making it so far the only design that retains this aspect of Libeskind's master plan. Maki clad the tower in colorless silver glass that reflects its surroundings (and throws shadows onto the memorial plaza) but also hides

the building's most remarkable feature: its structure. To achieve column-free spaces and corners, structural engineer Leslie E. Robertson designed two pairs of composite steel-and-concrete columns per elevation, placing them 20–45 feet (6–13.7 m) from the corners and threading them through the below-grade infrastructure. The column-pairs can be glimpsed behind the ultra-clear glass at the two-story lobby.

(Q) 3 World Trade Center

ROGERS STIRK HARBOUR + PARTNERS, 2018 – 175 GREENWICH STREET

To the north is 3WTC, designed by Richard Rogers for Silverstein Properties with 80 stories and a tip of 1,079 feet (328 m), about 90 feet (27 m) less than the original design, whose spires were removed in 2015. Like the shorter 4WTC, 3WTC rises with a few setbacks: its starts at the trapezoidal base with retail and large trading floors, has a square midsection, and then smaller rectangular footprints at the upper floors. But while the structure of 4WTC is hidden behind glass, 3WTC expresses its steel structure—at least the K-shaped bracing at the inset corners.

Walk north to the western tip of the 9/11 Museum.

(R) National September 11 Memorial Museum

SNØHETTA & DAVIS BRODY BOND, 2014 – 180 GREENWICH STREET

If the 9/11 Memorial can be seen as two beasts—pools and plaza—the same can be said for the 9/11 Memorial Museum. (Technically, the memorial and museum exist as one entity, the nonprofit National September 11 Memorial & Museum.) The museum is made up of an above-grade pavilion designed by Snøhetta and underground galleries designed by Davis Brody Bond. The former, situated just north of the memorial's south pool, is a glass-and-steel volume where every line and surface are angular, drawing comparisons to Libeskind's initial master plan proposal and making the pavilion as much his as Craig Dykers and his colleagues at Snøhetta. Stainless-steel panels lift to provide ingress to and egress from the museum on the north and south, respectively. At the western tip, metal gives way to an all-glass corner that frames two steel tridents recovered from Yamasaki's original towers. The rusty remnants stand 53 feet (16 m) tall and rise from the museum's lobby level to the pavilion's glass corner, uniting the museum's two architectural components.

While the below-grade museum that requires admission to gain entry falls outside of the scope of this walking tour, a few words on Davis Brody Bond's design. A visit to the museum is a descent into darkness followed by an ascent into light. Visitors descend

a ramp, which recalls the one used to haul debris out of WTC site after 9/11, and end up at the level of bedrock 70 feet (21 m) down. The spaces between the footprints of the towers are used for the display of large artifacts, such as the 36-foot-tall (11 m) "Large Column" emblazoned with memorial inscriptions, and displays the original slurry wall that keeps the Hudson River at bay (the WTC site, not just BPC, is landfill). The footprints proper contain the main multimedia exhibitions, where people can relive that horrific Tuesday minute by minute, or where younger people can learn it anew. It's an emotionally draining experience that is leavened once ascending back to plaza level.

⦂ *Walk to the western edge of the 9/11 Memorial's north pool.*

This spot affords a postcard view of Santiago Calatrava's birdlike WTC Transportation Hub [G]. Most dramatic are the 114 ribs, which follow the structure we saw earlier inside, cantilevering from the large Vierendeel truss that forms the skylight "spine." The asymmetry of the ribs imbues the building with movement, even as the steel structure—inside and out—weighs nearly 12,000 tons (10,886 tonnes).

The void in the skyline between 3WTC and One World Trade Center is slated for 2 World Trade Center. Originally designed by Foster + Partners with an angular, diamond-shaped crown, Bjarke Ingels Group (BIG) was brought on by Larry Silverstein when 21st Century Fox and News Corp tentatively agreed to anchor the 80-plus-story tower. BIG's design rose vertically at the corner facing the memorial but stepped in two directions in seven stacked volumes to create terraces facing east and overhangs on the north. The design was released in June 2015, but by January the following year Fox and News Corp pulled out of the project, delaying the WTC site's second-tallest tower until another anchor tenant can be found.

Another element to be completed at the north edge of the WTC site is the Ronald O. Perelman Center for Performing Arts, located immediately east of One World Trade Center. Frank Gehry's $400 million design for the site was shelved in 2014, and the following year REX, the firm led by Joshua Ramus, took over after winning an invited competition. REX's design is a lantern-like cube with walls made from marble laminated to glass. The three auditoriums inside would be accessed via grand stairs facing the memorial. The building—half the cost of Gehry's and expected to be completed in 2020—echoes the base of its much taller neighbor.

(S) ## One World Trade Center

SKIDMORE, OWINGS & MERRILL (SOM), 2015 – 285 FULTON STREET

Layered with more than four thousand vertical glass fins in front of horizontal steel slats, the delicate exterior of One World Trade Center's 186-foot-tall (56.7 m) base belies what it covers: concrete walls more than two feet (0.6 m) thick that protect the 60-foot-high (18.2 m) lobby from car bombs. It is a fortified base for a 94-story tower that regained the height lost on 9/11 and overcame the engineering deficiencies that brought down the Twin Towers. Yamasaki's towers, with their tightly spaced steel façades, were strong, but the relatively weak floors and cores meant a lack of redundancy. The structure of One WTC, engineered by WSP, on the other hand, has a concrete core with walls up to four feet (1.2 m) thick and 45,000 tons (40,823 tonnes) of steel at the perimeter. It's a redundant system that responds to the unavoidable fact that a 1,776-foot-tall (541 m) tower at Ground Zero is an open target.

That symbolic height—the year of the Declaration of Independence—came from Daniel Libeskind's "Memory Foundations," but that is all that remains of what he dubbed Freedom Tower. In the hands of SOM's David Childs, the original asymmetrical tower, meant to evoke the Statue of Liberty, gave way to a symmetrical form that recalls the Washington Monument. A 200-foot-square (18.5 sq m) plan tapers to a 150-foot-square (14 sq m) plan rotated 45 degrees, creating octagonal floor plates, each one unique. In effect, the all-glass exterior is made up of eight interlocking triangles; when seen from below, at the midpoint of one of the elevations, this creates the impression that the tower culminates in one point. In actuality, the metal-clad

lines of the triangles meet at a six-foot-tall (1.8 m) band at the roof—its upper elevation of 1,368 feet and lower elevation of 1,362 reference the original Twin Towers. To hit 1,776 feet (541 m), a 441-foot (41 m) mast rises from a series of circular communication platforms.

One WTC, created by a public-private partnership of the Port Authority and Durst Organization, contains three million square feet (278,709 sq m) of office space, a third of the ten million Larry Silverstein was responsible for after signing the 99-year lease in July 2001 (Silverstein pulled out of One WTC in 2006). Surrounded by millions of square feet of apartments in new and retrofitted towers, the World Trade Center site is an anomaly, a commercial island in an increasingly residential Lower Manhattan. Uniting them is a renewed public realm that, in parts, prioritizes people on foot over those in cars.

End of tour. Want to see more at the World Trade Center site? Walk into One World Trade Center to go up to One World Observatory. Or backtrack to R to visit the National September 11 Museum.

2 West Side Living

2.75 MILES / 4.4 KM

⟩ *This tour starts at the southwest corner of Leonard and Church Streets in Tribeca and ends in the West Village overlooking a remnant of the elevated railway that was transformed into the High Line.*

Early last century, industrial piers stretched up the Hudson River from the Battery to the Upper West Side. Most respectable New Yorkers shied away from the working waterfront and therefore lived toward the middle of the island. But in today's postindustrial Manhattan, the West Side is a highly desirable—and expensive—place, home to residential developments catering to the well-to-do who want to live close to the waterfront and its now recreational piers. Although this century's transformation of the West Side extends all the way up to, and past, 59th Street, this tour targets three neighborhoods south of 14th Street: Tribeca, Hudson Square, and the West Village.

The popular area now called Tribeca (Triangle Below Canal) first took its name from Washington Market, which operated as a wholesale produce market from the early 1800s all the way to the late 1950s (the market moved to the Bronx in the 1960s). With its well-preserved crop of commercial buildings, many of which catered to the market, Tribeca is now home to four NYC Historic Districts designated by the city's Landmarks Preservation Commission (LPC) in the early 1990s. This tour starts in a gap between three of those districts; as such, it is home to a building that towers over its neighbors.

 ## 56 Leonard Street
HERZOG & DE MEURON, 2017

With 57 floors that reach 821 feet (250 m) up, 56 Leonard is less than half the height of One World Trade Center [1S] a half mile (0.8 km) south. But with neighbors hovering around ten or twelve stories, the Jenga-like tower stands out in all directions. (The upward-craning perspective provides a good view of the base and middle sections, but we'll get a better view of its top later

BANK ST

END

PERRY ST

CHARLES ST

S

N R
O Q
P

WASHINGTON ST

M

LEROY ST

CLARKSON ST

L

WEST ST

HUDSON RIVER

SPRING ST

K

J I
H

RENWICK ST

G

CANAL ST

F

WATTS ST

VARICK ST

VESTRY ST

E

D
C

HUBERT ST

HUDSON ST

GRENWICH ST

B

FRANKLIN ST

CHURCH ST

LEONARD ST

A

START

A   56 Leonard Street
B   Unhistoric Townhouse
C   408 Greenwich Street
D   The Sterling Mason
E   V33
F   565 Broome SoHo
G   15 Renwick
H   497 Greenwich Street
I   512 Greenwich Street
J   Urban Glass House
K   Spring Street Salt Shed & Manhattan
    Districts 1/2/5 Garage
L   160 Leroy Street
M   Hudson River Park
N   173–176 Perry Street
O   165 Charles Street
P   150 Charles Street
Q   Carriage House
R   166 Perry Street
S   Superior Ink

(A)

in the tour.) Part of this disjunction in height arises from its location outside of a historic district, but it also arises from developer Alexico Group's purchase of air rights from the neighboring New York Law School (BKSK Architects, 2009), which formerly owned the 56 Leonard lot.

Alexico Group bought the site in 2006, but two years later the daring project appeared dead. Before the recession, developers had been hiring Pritzker Prize–winning architects (Jacques Herzog and Pierre de Meuron won in 2001) to design condo towers, using their celebrity status to set their projects apart. Not surprisingly, the recession killed quite a few of those projects. In 2012, 56 Leonard came back from the dead, wrapping up construction just over a decade after the tower's inception.

Herzog & de Meuron conceptualized the tower as a stack of individual houses—145 total—achieved through dramatic, asymmetrical cantilevers. Although a departure from the norm, the traditional tripartite composition of skyscrapers remains, since the cantilevers occur at the base and the top, while the middle of the tower is a simple extrusion enlivened by staggered balconies in varying widths. The concrete structure required numerous transfers to accommodate shifting columns and Vierendeel trusses for the longest cantilevers. A water-filled tank at the top of the building counteracts the winds acting upon the slender (1:10) tower.

Standing in the plaza-like space at the base of the building yields views into the dark-tile lobby and parking entrance to the side, but also a subtle and unique detail: the concave profile of the slab edges. Not present at the time of this writing is the proposed sculpture by Anish Kapoor, who bought an apartment in the tower in 2016. Recalling his polished, reflective *Cloud Gate* sculpture in Chicago, the unnamed piece will appear to be squashed by the tower—but also eat into the open space at the corner.

Walk west on Leonard Street past New York Law School at West Broadway to Hudson Street, turn right and make a quick left on Franklin Street.

(B) Unhistoric Townhouse

SYSTEM ARCHITECTS, 2018 – 187 FRANKLIN STREET

To cross Hudson Street is to enter the Tribeca West Historic District, established in 1991. Such a designation does not automatically bar atypical architecture though. Case in point is this five-story townhouse situated on a shallow lot only 25 feet (7.6 m) deep and 40 feet (12 m) wide. Architect Jeremy Edmiston renovated and expanded the previous structure, a three-story brick building with a grid of rectangular windows much like its neighbors. With the design approved by LPC in 2011, the new windows angle left and right between twisting expanses of brick that look more like fabric than masonry. Appearing as slits within the brick wall, the angled windows are meant to provide views for its residents up and down the street, all the while cutting down on views into the townhouse from the buildings across the street. The privacy is reinforced by some perforated metal balconies— alien appendages to the brick in line with this strange addition to the neighborhood.

Walk west to Greenwich Street, turn right and head north until you reach Hubert Street.

(C) 408 Greenwich Street
MORRIS ADJMI ARCHITECTS, 2008

This corner building sits on the southern edge of the Tribeca North Historic District (1992), on the site of an old garage. Built by an investment bank for its corporate headquarters, its top two floors serve as residences for the bank's executives, while rental apartments are tucked below it and retail on the ground floor rounds out the mix of uses. With its south façade given prominence due to the setback of Citigroup headquarters, the building works with its neighbor across Greenwich to form a gateway of sorts to the blocks of Tribeca North. In 2004, the city granted permission for more height and floor area than otherwise allowable, aligning it with the nine-story building across the street rather than its six-story neighbor to the west. The architect appears to have borrowed motifs from both of these buildings though, particularly the arched openings arrayed as two-story modules across the midsection of the two façades. These arches—made from pigmented precast concrete panels—are also found as shallow, double-wide openings at the base, echoing the neighbor across the street. The dark-gray metal used for the spandrel panels and canopies also caps the building, where small windows with arched openings recall its neighbor to the west. Last in this mishmash of historical elements are the round terracotta columns at the corner that spell out the street names just above head height and accentuate the importance of the corner.

Walk up one block to Laight Street and turn left on the north side of the street.

(D) The Sterling Mason
MORRIS ADJMI ARCHITECTS, 2016 – 71 LAIGHT STREET

Immediately north of 408 Greenwich is another Adjmi building occupying the former site of another garage. Although the building looks like it has always been there, it is actually a copy—more accurately, a mirror image of the 1905 warehouse building to the west. From across the street the resemblance is uncanny: everything is the same but the color. A closer look—and feel, recommended (cross the street to do so)—reveals that the gray bricks aren't bricks at all (they are plasma-finished GFRC [glass fiber reinforced concrete]) and the "stone" base is aluminum. Otherwise, the copy is precise down to a fraction of an inch (note the vertical grooves and rounded bullnoses in the aluminum/stone bases), made possible by measuring the old building by hand and with laser scanners. Behind the exterior walls of metal, concrete, and brick are 33 condominium units across seven floors—further uniting the original and copy.

Return to Greenwich Street, turn left and head north to Vestry Street and turn right.

(E) V33

ARCHI-TECTONICS, 2011 – 33 VESTRY STREET

About as far from a copy as could be, yet still sitting within the Tribeca North Historic District, is this nine-story residential building designed by the firm of Winka Dubbeldam. The seven single- and multi-floor units are hidden behind a random pattern of glass and stone—hidden because the façade's busy composition denies an understanding of the building's layout, unlike the traditional windows of its neighbors. Glass is alternately clear and translucent, and stone alternates between opaque and translucent, making the building's expression at night truly revealing. Occupying a former surface parking lot, the building fills a void long in need of being filled. But it also creates a void: in the form of a terrace, the one space where the lives of the residents makes an appearance on the outside of the building.

Continue east to Hudson Street, turn left up the east side of the street and cross Canal Street to Watts Street.

The Holland Tunnel, dating back to 1927, comes above ground and connects to the city in two spots, cutting up parts of Tribeca and Hudson Square: exit ramps are just south of Canal Street and entry ramps are just north of where we are standing. In recent years that development has pushed farther west, such that condos now overlook the entrance to the Holland Tunnel.

Look east across Varick Street.

(F) 565 Broome SoHo

RENZO PIANO BUILDING WORKSHOP (RPBW), 2018

Although this condo development sits in Hudson Square, the industrial area once known as the Printing District, Bizzi & Partners Development's inclusion of SoHo in the name points to the blurring of neighborhood designations in this swath of Lower Manhattan. Regardless, Hudson Square does not have the cachet as the historic cast iron district to the east; the neighborhood's lack of any landmark districts means its blocks have been targeted for large residential developments following a 2013 rezoning of nearly twenty blocks in Hudson Square. Piano's project is on the larger end of the spectrum, with two 30-story towers housing 115 apartments. The curtain wall with low-iron glass is hardly groundbreaking, but the slender frames and curved-glass corners make it stand out from other all-glass buildings in the city.

(F)

Walk east on Watts Street—stopping at Varick Street to look south for a great view of the top of 56 Leonard Street [A]— then cross Varick to get a closer look at 565 Broome SoHo.

The steel mullions and rounded corners are vivid up close, as are a few other details that were still under construction at the time of writing: the curved-glass returns that give the units more corners than typical rectangular floor plates; the way the gap between towers is enclosed by ultra-clear glass at the lower floors and connected by a decorative structure at their roofs; and the private driveway tucked into the east end of the site— what's become a standard amenity in residential developments that carry the name of a Pritzker Prize–winning architect.

Walk up Varick Street alongside the Dominick (formerly known as the Trump SoHo), turn left on Spring Street and head west. Take another left at Renwick Street to about halfway down the block.

(G) 15 Renwick

ODA NEW YORK, 2016

A trio of blocks north of Canal Street has seen an enormous amount of residential development this century, due in part to the rezoning of three blocks west of Hudson Street and south of Spring Street in 2003 from manufacturing to commercial, which allows residential uses. The location of these blocks at a remove from the Holland Tunnel also helps, keeping them quiet and secluded, creating the feeling of a residential enclave. A highlight on Renwick Street, where at least five other developments can be found, is this 11-story building with 31 residences designed by Eran Chen's ODA for Izaki Group Investments. On this and other projects, Chen has exploited the city's dormer rule, which allows some floor area at the top of the building to penetrate a required zoning setback above the maximum base height. Here the allowable dormers are distributed asymmetrically across the top three floors to create a variety of outdoor "rooms" for the penthouse units. Townhouse units, behind the copper panels at the base of the building, have their own backyards. While the apartments in the middle of the building don't have their own private outdoor spaces (they share a rooftop terrace), the deep-set wood and aluminum windows they look out through create one of the most handsome façades around.

(G)

Continue down to Canal Street, turn right and at the next corner turn right up Greenwich Street to halfway up the west side of the block.

(H) 497 Greenwich Street

ARCHI-TECTONICS, 2004

Writing about Winka Dubbeldam's design in the *New York Times* three years before it would be completed, Herbert Muschamp called 497 Greenwich a "parabuilding." Her eleven-story glass addition to a six-story brick loft building is very much like a parasite, sitting next to and on top of its neighbor, as if the older building were a host it depended upon. But more exciting than the engagement of new and old—a subtle relationship given the setback on the upper floors and the shifting architectural climate in the years since—is the rippling glass façade made of both flat and curved panes of glass. Gaps in the horizontal fins draw our eyes to the curved glass section, where the façade angles back gently instead of stepping back abruptly, as is the norm in buildings brick and glass alike. 497 Greenwich remains one of the most daring NYC buildings from the first decade of the twenty-first century; even the newer glass building next door (by Handel Architects) cannot diminish its parasitic punch.

⋮ *Walk up to Spring Street and cross to the east side.*

(I) 512 Greenwich Street
ARCHI-TECTONICS, 2018

A decade and a half after Winka Dubbeldam's undulating façade of glass was completed down the block, she returned to Greenwich Street to design another residential "parabuilding": a six-story single-family townhouse that adds three floors to a four-story industrial loft building. But any distinction between the new floors and the structurally reinforced old ones is blurred by the porous screen that starts above the ground-floor retail and wraps the townhouse and its outdoor terraces like a veil. Projecting from the screen is a large window at the top floor, a unique view of the city framed for the residents.

⋮ *Cross Spring Street to get a better view of the north side*
⋮ *of 512 Greenwich, then walk west one block to the northwest*
⋮ *corner of Washington Street.*

(J) Urban Glass House
PHILIP JOHNSON & ANNABELLE SELLDORF, 2006 – 330 SPRING STREET

In the same 2001 article where Herbert Muschamp commended Winka Dubbeldam's Greenwich Street "parabuilding," the architecture critic lavished praise over what would be the last creation of one of his favorite architects: Philip Johnson. He called the 12-story building with 50 condos for CB Developers "a symbolic gateway to the downtown state of mind." But in the dozen years since Johnson created the Urban Glass House (he died in 2005 and would not see it completed), the building became a footnote on his long career rather than an exclamation point, unlike the famous Glass House from 1949 this building's name references. Architect Annabelle Selldorf designed the interiors, but the grid of windows reflects its surroundings rather than offering any glimpses inside.

(K) Spring Street Salt Shed & Manhattan Districts 1/2/5 Garage

DATTNER ARCHITECTS & WXY, 2015 – 336/353 SPRING STREET

This nearly decade-long project, designed by Dattner Architects with WXY, is made up of a large five-story garage north of Spring Street housing more than 150 garbage trucks and the diminutive Salt Shed positioned on an otherwise unusable wedge of land across the street. Architecturally they are an odd pair: the rectilinear garage covered in more than 2,600 perforated metal fins and the angular salt shed shaped like a salt crystal in exposed concrete. Their differences are united by the goals of hiding their contents—be they garbage trucks or a 5,000-ton (4,356 tonnes), 40-foot-high (12 m) mound of deicing salt— and pleasing the current and future residents of Hudson Square through architectural quality aligned with New York City's Department of Design and Construction's Design and Construction Excellence 2.0 program and the Public Design Commission.

Walk to the northeast corner of West Street for a good view of the Salt Shed. Then head down West Street to Canal Street and east to the building's Department of Sanitation (DSNY) gate.

Accessed by a huge 34-foot-tall (10.3 m) door facing a gated yard to the east, the salt shed is completely closed off on the other sides; in fact, it is the first salt shed in the city to be fully enclosed. Walls of concrete six feet (1.8 m) thick ascend to a height of 69 feet (21 m) at a prow-like corner facing the river. The stacked joints are eight feet (2.4 m) tall, reflecting the height of the pours that took place in the summer of 2015.

Continue east to Washington Street, cross to the south fork of Canal Street on the other side of the small, triangular Canal Park, and then walk west across West Street into Hudson River Park [M]. *Turn right and head north to the cobblestone area just past the basketball court.*

A view of the NYC Department of Sanitation (DSNY) buildings from Hudson River Park makes it clear their appearance from the west was important for Dattner and WXY. The salt shed looks like a contemporary foil to the Holland Tunnel exhaust building behind it, while the garage cloaks itself behind metal panels, graced with the DSNY logo at one corner. At night, the salt shed's uplights give it an ominous presence, while the color-coded floors of the garage (corresponding to the three districts it serves) can be read on its south façade.

Seeing these two buildings from the linear Hudson River Park is fitting since the park led, in part, to their creation. The consolidation of three district garages into one came after a 2005 settlement between the city and Friends of Hudson River Park for the removal of the garbage trucks from the 8-acre (3.2 ha) peninsula at Gansevoort Street one mile (1.6 km) north of here. The peninsula is slated to become part of Hudson River Park, complete with a beach, play lawn, and boating areas.

Continue north up the Hudson River Park to Pier 40 and cross West Street at Clarkson Street.

(L) 160 Leroy Street

HERZOG & DE MEURON, 2018

Not surprisingly, Manhattan's rectangular blocks lead most architects to create rectilinear buildings. Numerous instances veer from the right angle, with a few of them found overlooking landscapes: at Central Park (Frank Lloyd Wright's Guggenheim Museum), at Battery Park (the curved glass façade of 17 State Street), or here at Hudson River Park. Swiss architects Jacques Herzog and Pierre de Meuron, who experimented with cantilevered boxes in Tribeca [A], channel the curves of Oscar Niemeyer and Morris Lapidus in this corner of the West Village. Paired with developer Ian Schrager once again [4E, 4G],

Herzog & de Meuron placed the 57 residences on 14 floors
behind rounded corners and a concave façade overlooking
Hudson River Park. Set back from the deep-set concrete structure
are faceted floor-to-ceiling windows, an angular counterpoint
to the undulating curves. More Miami Beach than Manhattan,
160 Leroy Street is aligned with the waves it looks upon rather
than the block it sits upon.

Walk up to Leroy Street and walk halfway down the block
to glance into the building's private courtyard.

Not all the units face the water. Some face the nearly
10,000-square-foot (929 sq m) private courtyard by garden
designer Madison Cox. With all residents entering into the
courtyard from Leroy Street, the landscape—oriented about
a transported mature willow tree—acts as a buffer between
the city outside and the apartments within.

Backtrack to West Street, walk north one block to
Morton Street, cross West Street into Hudson River Park,
and walk north to Pier 45.

(M) Hudson River Park

ABEL BAINNSON BUTZ (ABB), 2003

Extending five miles (8 km), from Battery Park to 59th Street,
Hudson River Park offers 500 acres (202 ha) of recreation where

the shipping industry once thrived. Attempts to build a park in place of the piers goes back to the early 1970s and Westway, a scheme to bury a highway in landfill and top it with green space. That plan died in 1985, after a drawn-out fight between politicians, community groups, and environmentalists. The city's comprehensive waterfront plan from 1992 and the signing of the Hudson River Park Act five years later led to its replacement: a linear park separated from the adjacent neighborhoods by the six-lane West Street (in place of the elevated highway that was demolished after a section collapsed on its own in 1973).

Hudson River Park's master plan was created by a team led by Quennell Rothschild & Partners, but smaller sections were designed by other firms and realized intermittently since a section adjacent to the West Village was completed in 1999. The first formal dedication took place in 2003, for the section between Leroy and Jane Streets designed by ABB with a slew of consultants. Like other Hudson River Park designers, ABB worked with the community group inland from their site to determine amenities, here including a promenade, lawns, seating areas, a playground, a dog run, restrooms, and concessions. The strongest feature of ABB's contribution to the park is Pier 45, 860 feet (262 m) long and supported by 1,200 concrete pilings. Groves of locust trees at both ends of the pier provide shade, while expanses of lawn and plenty of benches invite relaxation and taking in the skyline.

Walk halfway down the north side of Pier 45 for a view of the towers along West Street.

(N) 173–176 Perry Street
RICHARD MEIER & PARTNERS ARCHITECTS, 2002

Even though Richard Meier won the Pritzker Architecture Prize in 1984, becoming the sixth laureate of architecture's "Nobel," the New York City architect would not realize his first ground-up building in Manhattan until 2002, when a pair of glass towers went up at the west end of Perry Street in the West Village. CB Developers hired Meier to design the 15-story towers. In turn he created generous windows overlooking the Hudson, accommodated by placing the concrete core on the east. Each floor is given over to a single unit (about 3,500 square feet [352 sq m] in 176 Charles Street on the south and 1,800 square feet [167 sq m] in the smaller 173 Charles Street on the north), though some of the raw, loftlike floors were combined; Meier himself designed a huge triplex in the south tower, complete with a spiral stair that's sometimes visible behind the glass façade—depending if the curtains are drawn to shield the interiors from the hot western sun.

N
O

O 165 Charles Street

RICHARD MEIER & PARTNERS ARCHITECTS, 2006

The success and influence of the Perry Street towers was immediate. But when it came time to extend the row of glass towers one more block, Meier did so for a different developer: Alexico Group, the company behind 56 Leonard Street [A]. The architect seemed to have learned some lessons from the first two towers: he ditched the superfluous white grid on the west elevation; the frosted glass guardrails at the balconies changed to clear glass; most of the floors feature two units (31 in total) and were laid out by the architect rather than left as raw space; and the elevator core on the east is covered in glass, making it a better neighbor to the low-rise buildings behind it. Even with these subtle details, the 16-story tower at 165 Charles Street certainly makes a trio with the earlier pair.

Walk north up the Hudson River Park and cross West Street at Charles Street.

(P) # 150 Charles Street

COOKFOX, 2015

In 2005, as Meier's third tower was under construction, the city approved a rezoning of the "Far West Village" to promote the residential development west of Washington Street, but at heights consistent with the existing low-scale fabric. A couple of spots were excluded from the area's downsizing: the block north of Bethune Street (where Superior Ink [S] is located) and the block south of Charles Street behind the newly designated Weehawken Street Historic District. The latter is where the large 150 Charles Street development, with 91 condos for Witkoff, is located. In response to the presence of the historic district, the incorporation of parts of the old Whitehall Storage warehouse into the project, and the Hudson River just one block away, COOKFOX's building rises to a contextual crescendo of brick and glass toward Washington Street on the east. The townhouses along Charles and West 10th Streets feature large casement windows between a grid of brick piers, the reused structural frame of the old warehouse. Behind the frames and above the townhouses are two "legs" that ascend, Sphinx-like, to the 16-story tower.

Walk east to Washington Street then right to the middle of the block.

Here, in the gap between two of the West Village Houses completed in 1975, is a peek at an all-glass façade of the development's tower.

Walk north up Washington Street then left up Charles Lane.

(Q) # Carriage House

CHRISTOFF : FINIO, 2006 – 12 CHARLES LANE

The angular glass façade of Asymptote's 166 Perry Street [R] may scream for attention on this narrow cobblestone lane between

Charles and Perry Streets, but just opposite it is this little gem, a two-story carriage house at the rear of an old brick townhouse. When a fire damaged the old carriage house, the owner of the townhouse hired architects Taryn Christoff and Martin Finio to design a modern unit he could rent out. The upstairs glass wall echoes the Meier towers just steps away, but the twisted pickets of the ground floor are one of a kind. They conceal the entrance and screen the shallow outdoor space for storage on this narrow lane.

Walk west on Charles Lane, turn right up West Street, and then right on the north side of Perry Street.

(R) ## 166 Perry Street
ASYMPTOTE ARCHITECTURE, 2010

Although the folded glass curtain wall of this eight-story condo building may signal new construction, in fact it is the conversion and expansion of a six-story parking garage owned by CB Developers, which had tapped Meier for the adjacent Perry Street towers [N] and used the garage to serve those residents. But cars gave way to more residents, as architects Lise Anne Couture and Hani Rashid were brought on board in 2006 (one year after the developer added two floors themselves to beat the area's downzoning) to design a new exterior and interiors for 27 apartments. The glass façades facing Perry Street and Charles Lane angle in and out, as if the younger architects are levying a

critique at Meier's button-down Modernism. Whatever the case, the angled planes are best seen from further east and closer to sunset, when they reflect the golden sky over Hudson River Park.

Walk to West Street, turn right and walk north to Bethune Street, then right until opposite the townhouses on the north side of the street.

(S) Superior Ink

ROBERT A.M. STERN ARCHITECTS (RAMSA), 2009 –
400 WEST 12TH STREET

Although Related Companies did not preserve the Superior Ink factory as part of its plans for this large condo development— unlike 150 Charles Street [P] with the Whitehall Storage building—the developer did, obviously, co-opt the name. Built by Nabisco in 1919, the low-rise factory was occupied by Superior Ink from 1981 until 2006, when it moved to New Jersey. While the factory is long gone, architect Robert A.M. Stern designed a 15-story tower that is a neo-traditional echo of its predecessor; this occurs through its massing, particularly the three-story base, and the articulation of its brick façade, with arched windows and large expanses of glass facing the Hudson River. An extension of the project along Bethune Street consists of seven townhouses, each one different— their neo-Georgian details more London than West Village.

Behind you, walk up the steps and through the portal to the courtyard of Westbeth Artists Housing.

From the late 1800s to the mid-1960s, this block served as the headquarters of Bell Telephone Laboratories. Although the agglomeration of buildings would not be designated a NYC landmark until 2011, the rise of the preservation movement and displacement of artists in the 1960s combined to create Westbeth Artists Housing, completed in 1970. Richard Meier's first major public project is most visible in the courtyard, which was formed by the removal of a roof and two floors and is punctuated by curved balconies.

Walk south out of the courtyard to Bank Street, then left to the southeast corner of Washington Street.

This tour ends with a view of two important developments. Stretching to the south, along the west side of Washington Street, is West Village Houses, which we glimpsed earlier. Although the architecture, by Perkins+Will, is unremarkable—dreary and monotonous, even—the affordable housing project, completed in 1975, is a notable hinge from mid-century, slum-clearance projects promoted by longtime planning commissioner Robert Moses to contextual plans inspired by Jane Jacobs's *Death and Life of Great American Cities* from 1961. Jacobs, a West Village resident until 1968, had a hand in shaping West Village Houses, whose five-story walk-ups were considered a reaction to the towers-in-the-park favored by the city at the time. The 42 buildings with 420 affordable units occupy the right of way of the elevated freight rail—now known as the High Line—whose section south of Bank Street was demolished in 1963.

A remnant of the High Line, whose section from Bethune to Gansevoort Streets came down in 1991, is visible on top of and within a couple of the old Bell Labs buildings from the 1920s and 30s. This one-block chunk of the High Line is all that remains of the elevated railway beyond the footprint of the popular park, making this spot a fitting segue to the next tour.

| *End of tour. The walking tour of the High Line* [TOUR 3] *is just five short blocks up Washington Street.*

3 High Line and Its Environs

⟩ *This tour starts at sidewalk level beneath the southern tip
of the High Line and ends beyond the northern tip of the
park at the new 34th Street–Hudson Yards subway station.*

A familiar legend tells us that the elevated railway supporting the popular High Line park was "saved" in 1999. That was the year two interested citizens, Joshua David and Robert Hammond, met at a community meeting, discovered they were the only people in the crowd who didn't want to demolish the structure, and months later founded the nonprofit Friends of the High Line (FHL). The reality of rescuing the structure and creating the elevated park is, obviously, much more complicated, as are the circumstances that led to this twenty-first-century phenomenon.

A century and a half before the fateful meeting between David and Hammond, the city of New York laid down surface tracks next to the industrial piers, warehouses, and factories lining the Hudson River. The avenues on Manhattan's West Side promptly became known as "Death Avenue," which required "West Side Cowboys" to gallop on horseback in front of the freight trains to warn pedestrians, prompting an 1866 State Senate Committee to call the tracks "an evil which has already been endured too long [15 years] and must be speedily abated." This bureaucratic "speediness" took nearly sixty years: in 1934 the elevated railroad running from West 34th Street down to Clarkson Street officially opened. The rail structure's operational life would be markedly shorter than its gestation period, with the section south of Bank Street chopped off in the early 1960s and the last train running along its surface in 1980. The section south of Gansevoort Street came down in 1991, the last major change to the structure before the 1999 community meeting.

It's easy to grasp the appeal of the High Line, which ran train cars three stories above grade in the blocks *between* the avenues rather than *above* them. This mid-block condition meant in its heyday the High Line directly served industrial buildings through spurs or by actually penetrating buildings, but it also complicated the railway's demolition. This melding of architecture

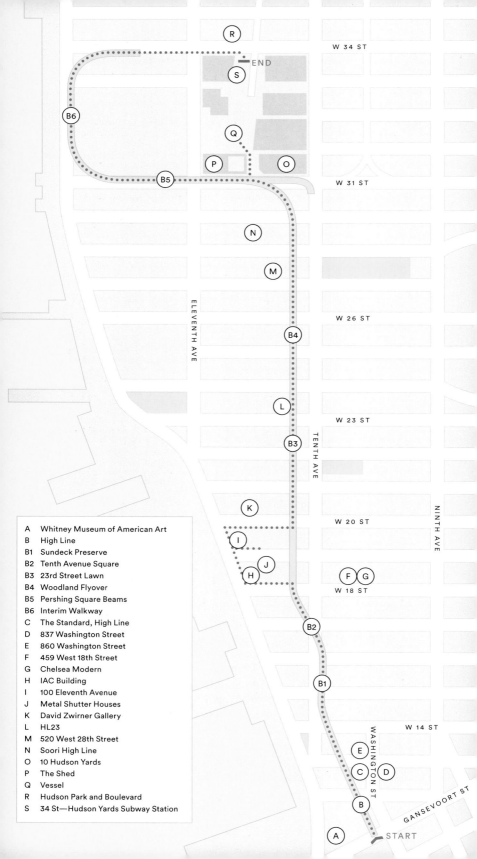

W 34 ST

R

END

S

B6

Q

P O

W 31 ST

B5

N

M

ELEVENTH AVE

W 26 ST

B4

L

W 23 ST

B3

TENTH AVE

K

W 20 ST

I

NINTH AVE

J

H

F G

W 18 ST

B2

B1

W 14 ST

E

WASHINGTON ST

C D

B

GANSEVOORT ST

A

START

A   Whitney Museum of American Art
B   High Line
B1   Sundeck Preserve
B2   Tenth Avenue Square
B3   23rd Street Lawn
B4   Woodland Flyover
B5   Pershing Square Beams
B6   Interim Walkway
C   The Standard, High Line
D   837 Washington Street
E   860 Washington Street
F   459 West 18th Street
G   Chelsea Modern
H   IAC Building
I   100 Eleventh Avenue
J   Metal Shutter Houses
K   David Zwirner Gallery
L   HL23
M   520 West 28th Street
N   Soori High Line
O   10 Hudson Yards
P   The Shed
Q   Vessel
R   Hudson Park and Boulevard
S   34 St—Hudson Yards Subway Station

and transportation appealed to David and Hammond but not to the Chelsea Property Owners (CPO), who saw the structure as an impediment to maximizing their property values, and therefore demanded its demolition. With the support of Mayor Rudy Giuliani, the CPO was Goliath to FHL's David. But FHL had a number of factors in their favor: celebrities who found the structure appealing gave money to the nonprofit; stunning photographs by Joel Sternfeld published in the *New Yorker* (May 2001) revealed a ready-made park in the sky; and a spate of mayoral candidates in the 2001 election backed the structure's reuse as a public park. One of Giuliani's last acts as mayor was signing the High Line's demolition papers, but a judge effectively nullified the demolition permit, making the future of the High Line as a park rosy. Additionally, a study around the time concluded that an elevated park would pay back its cost of construction more than two-fold through tax revenues; a Certificate of Interim Trail Use was in hand in 2005; and CSX Transportation donated the majority of the High Line's length to the city in November of that year (the section north of 30th Street was donated in 2012). The Bloomberg administration enacted two initiatives to help the park pay off even more and reshape the blocks around it: rezoning much of the area from manufacturing to commercial to allow residential development, and the creation of a special district where air rights on properties adjacent to the High Line could be shifted to properties elsewhere in the district. Although the latter was intended to ensure sunlight would reach the park's surface, it also appeased the owners of properties alongside the High Line who could make money by selling their unused air rights.

The design of the 1.5-mile-long (2.4 km) High Line park was decided in a 2004 competition won by landscape architecture firm James Corner Field Operations with architecture firm Diller Scofidio + Renfro (DS+R). Finding inspiration in the "self-sown park" that bloomed in the decades following the railway's abandonment, the design team focused on "wild" and native plant species, developing a paving system that knit the landscape and hardscape together, and incorporating the structure's railroad tracks into the design to maintain the essence of its past. The park was realized and opened in three sections: Gansevoort Street to West 20th Street (2009); West 20th Street to West 30th Street (2011); and West 30th Street to its end at West 34th Street just west of Eleventh Avenue (2014).

 ## Whitney Museum of American Art

RENZO PIANO BUILDING WORKSHOP (RPBW), 2015 –
99 GANSEVOORT STREET

An integral element in the competition-winning design was an arts institution anchoring the southern end of the High Line.

Dia Art Foundation, the trailblazing nonprofit that moved from SoHo to Chelsea in 1987, was slated to make the move but pulled out in 2006, opening the door for the Whitney Museum of American Art. The Whitney had tried unsuccessfully with three architects—Michael Graves in the 1980s, Rem Koolhaas in the 1990s, and Renzo Piano in the 2000s—to expand its Marcel Breuer home on the Upper East Side. Piano's conservative expansion design gained approval from the Landmarks Preservation Commission (LPC), but the Whitney signed on in late 2006 to build a brand-new museum on the Dia site rather than spend any more time on expanding its Breuer building. (The Whitney still owns its Breuer building, leasing it to the Metropolitan Museum of Art.)

Upon its opening, critics lambasted the blue-metal museum's external appearance as clunky and more industrial than museum-like. Its massing arises from the desire to give the Whitney the largest column-free gallery in the city: a massive, 18,000-square-foot (1,672 sq m) space that recalls some of the Chelsea art galleries along the High Line—only larger and lifted five stories above sidewalk level. Above that level are more galleries on progressively smaller floor plates as well as outdoor terraces that step back from the High Line to ensure the park's plants and trees get plenty of sunlight. Below the large fifth-floor gallery are a glazed lobby, shop, and restaurant—all beneath a ceiling that angles up toward the High Line to visually connect the museum and elevated park. Although the building is an odd lump from the outside, the galleries and terraces are superior spaces for looking at art.

Ascend to the High Line and stop near the Diller –
von Furstenberg Building, which Piano designed with public
restrooms and service facilities for the High Line.

(B) ## High Line

FIELD OPERATIONS & DILLER SCOFIDIO + RENFRO (DS+R), 2009

The design of the High Line is basically a kit of parts that is broken up occasionally, like pearls on a string, by what I call "special moments." This tour highlights those moments and the new buildings that have sprung up alongside the park, but first a rundown of the kit that covers most of its length. First are the modular, precast concrete <u>planks</u>, one foot (30 cm) wide, with hollow joints between them to allow water to flow into the cavity between the planks and the existing concrete structure. At the planting beds the planks do two things: they taper to comb the hardscape and softscape together; and they rise up slightly to make people aware of these "edges" through their steps. Given that the High Line is suited to strolling, the subtle change in the height of the tapered planks grabs the attention of even the most lackadaisical visitor. Although these edges proved to be tripping hazards and are now accompanied by short ropes to visually alert people of the interface between hard and soft, the tapered planks make it clear that the walking surface, and our awareness of it, is important throughout the park. Second are the <u>benches</u> that appear to peel up from the planks. Instead of concrete, wood slats are used for the seating surfaces and occasional backs, making them warm and soft to the touch rather than cold and hard. Third is the <u>lighting</u>, a multifaceted design (by L'Observatoire International) that points light downward to the walking surfaces and the plants rather than up into the night sky. LED lights are located beneath stainless-steel hoods at the historic railings, in tubular fixtures about a foot (30 cm) above the walkway in straightaways, and as vertical tubes in some of the planting beds. Fourth are the original railroad <u>tracks</u>, which were labeled, removed during repair of the structure, and reinstalled within the planting beds and sometimes between the planks. The yellow labels, which can still be seen in places, allowed the tracks to be reinstalled in their original positions. Fifth and last are the <u>plantings</u>, which were chosen by James Corner with Dutch planting designer Piet Oudolf to be low-maintenance, diverse, and of interest at almost any time of the year. Sitting astride and combing into the walkways, the plantings sit in one to three feet (30–90 cm) of soil on top of filter fabric, drainage mats, root blockers, insulation, and other layers that go into making what is basically a really long planted bridge. Although the planting design is too varied and complex to go into any detail here, it's worth noting that the plants are trimmed in early spring, so a visit too soon in the season yields a short, thinned landscape, but soon after the native plants and flowers bloom quickly and beautifully.

(c) The Standard, High Line

ENNEAD ARCHITECTS, 2009 – 848 WASHINGTON STREET

One of the most surprising sights when walking up the stairs from Gansevoort Street for the first time is the view ahead—not of trees but of a building straddling the High Line. Unlike the early industrial buildings that seemed to merge themselves with the elevated structure, the Standard just stands over it, propped up on huge concrete legs on either side of the park. Behind the glass curtain wall that starts about 60 feet (18 m) above the street are hotel rooms for hotelier André Balazs. As designed by Ennead's Todd Schliemann, the tower slab kinks in the middle as if enjoying some liberty from the Manhattan grid; the bend is functional though, as it squeezes in one more hotel room per floor. Opening the same year as Section 1 of the High Line (the hotel immediately became known as a "voyeur's delight" for the naked bodies seen through glass), the Standard is the first twenty-first-century building to be built completely over the elevated park, since construction of both happened at the same time.

Walk north toward the Standard and stop beneath it.

A door-sized opening visible in the concrete leg captures a time when a public/private connection was envisioned as a possibility. A bridge would have connected hotel stair and High Line, but the city opted for controlled public access points—stairs every two or three blocks and elevators more sporadically—but no private access from neighboring properties.

(d) 837 Washington Street

MORRIS ADJMI ARCHITECTS, 2014

In 2003 an assemblage of blocks between the High Line and Hudson Street were designated the Gansevoort Market Historic District. The designation came out of a bottom-up movement of community leaders who wanted to preserve the area's distinct industrial architecture and deter any oversize developments. Most overt was restaurateur Florent Morellet, whose 24-hour French diner, Florent, opened in 1985, when trucks carrying beef carcasses rolled down the cobblestone streets during the day and transvestite prostitutes strolled them at night. Morellet was able to preserve the area's distinctive low-scale character, but he could not save his restaurant, which shuttered in 2008 after his rent increased sevenfold in one year. The area's astronomical rents mean tenants such as Samsung occupy buildings in the Meatpacking District instead of actual meat-packers. In 2016, the South Korean maker of smartphones, TVs, and other electronic devices opened its Samsung 837 "digital playground and marketing center" in this building sitting inside the historic district. It is an oddity, almost schizophrenic: steel-framed office floors twist as they rise from a two-story base with preserved brick walls and a wraparound canopy that used to shelter the back end of trucks but now shades window-shoppers.

(E) 860 Washington Street
JAMES CARPENTER DESIGN ASSOCIATES, 2016

The lot kitty-corner to Adjmi's postindustrial expressionism sits just outside of the historic district and therefore yields a modern, glassy building. James Carpenter, who excels in the engineering and effects of glass, designed a two-story retail base capped by nine office floors—all sheathed in crystal clear glass curtain walls. The base fills out the rectangular site (a portion literally extending beneath the High Line), while the office floors have a parallelogram shape to follow the angle of the High Line.

West of 860 Washington, on the other side of the High Line, is architect Jeanne Gang's Solar Carve tower and beyond it, in the Hudson River, is Thomas Heatherwick's off-again, on-again Pier 55, both under construction at the time of writing.

Walk north, take a right at the fork in the High Line just past 14th Street and then stop alongside the wooden chaises.

(B1) Sundeck Preserve, 2009

The designers call this first "special moment" the Sundeck Preserve for good reason: once the afternoon sun moves past the neighboring loft, people flock to the chaises to soak up the sun's rays. (Its official name is the Diller – von Furstenberg Sundeck after the husband-wife donors, who each have offices in the area.) Deeper than the typical peel-up benches, the chaises are perfect for reclining and are therefore often occupied by people taking in the sun and views. Across from the seating is a water feature so shallow that one can walk across it with sandals and retain dry feet. Water is introduced in a trough alongside the planted edge, skims along the concrete surface (with sealed, not open joints), and disappears into the one-foot-wide (30 cm) drain that fits seamlessly into the modular walkway. With no playground on the High Line until West 30th Street (in Section 3), this is a popular spot for kids to take their shoes off and splash around.

Walk north to the passage through Chelsea Market—the former Nabisco factory now home to a popular food market downstairs and tech companies upstairs—and continue to the next "moment," where the High Line traverses Tenth Avenue.

(B2) Tenth Avenue Square, 2009

Until this point, every footstep has been atop the High Line's modular concrete planks. At Tenth Avenue Square, concrete gives way to wood, a signal that something special is, literally, afoot. Facing north is a sunken amphitheater cut *into* the High Line's structure, culminating in large windows looking up the avenue. Part of the amphitheater's success stems from the accessible route winding back and forth between the wooden seats. This zigzag adds so much length to the ramp and makes its angle so shallow that, per the ADA (Americans with Disabilities Act), it is technically a slope rather than a ramp. Legally the latter would require railings (just like the adjacent stairs), but slopes do not, so here the view up the avenue is free of obstructions. Filling out the rest of Tenth Avenue Square is a small grove that intersperses trees with peel-up benches, the latter made entirely out of wood as an extension of the wood walkway. While the amphitheater looks north, the grove looks south to a distant view of the Statue of Liberty framed by a planted spur and an enclosed bridge spanning across Tenth Avenue.

Head north a few steps past Tenth Avenue Square.

When the first section of the High Line opened in 2009, the view here opened up into a wide panorama spanning from Chelsea Piers and a cluster of buildings by Pritzker Prize–winning architects (Frank Gehry, Jean Nouvel, and Shigeru Ban) on the left to a mix of old and new residential buildings across Tenth Avenue on the right. This expansiveness is short lived, though, as two projects started to rise at the time of this writing: two twisting towers designed by Bjarke Ingels Group (BIG) on the large site to the west, and across 18th Street two buildings by Thomas Heatherwick flanking the High Line.

(F)   ## 459 West 18th Street
DELLA VALLE + BERNHEIMER, 2009

East of Tenth Avenue are two neighbors vying for the attention of park-goers. On the left is an 11-story condo building developed *and* designed by Jared Della Valle and Andrew Bernheimer (the former now heads Alloy Development and the latter his eponymous architecture firm). I liken the two-tone design to a black-and-white cookie in building form, though the contrasting colors of aluminum panels actually articulate the two different zoning districts that cut the site in half, one allowing a taller volume than the other.

(G)   ## Chelsea Modern
AUDREY MATLOCK ARCHITECT, 2009 – 447 WEST 18TH STREET

459's neighbor, designed by Audrey Matlock, is about the same height as the white mass but rendered in horizontal bands of blue-glass curtain wall that zigzag across the front of the 12-story building. This mismatched pair perfectly expresses the precrisis moment when developers used attention-getting architecture— even in relatively small buildings such as these—to stand out from the crowd.

> *Descend the stairs at 18th Street and head west along the north side of the street, stopping near the entrance to the IAC Building.*

(H)   ## IAC Building
GEHRY PARTNERS, 2007 – 555 WEST 18TH STREET

Frank Gehry realized his first building in New York City for Barry Diller, the head of media company IAC/InterActiveCorp and husband of fashion designer Diane von Furstenberg and, along with his wife, one of the biggest donors to FHL. The massing of the ten-story building, which responds directly to the NYC building code setbacks, is apparent from the High Line, but up close one can grasp what gives the flowing glass its milky texture. Each

of the more than 1,300 unique panels of glass are covered with gradients of white dots—ceramic frits baked onto the insulated glass—denser toward the top and bottom in order to conceal the concrete structure, cut down on sunlight entering IAC's office spaces, and retain views for employees. This technique gives the building a recognizable, if gauzy, banding during the day, while after sundown the building glows softly like a lantern. More remarkable than the frits is the fact the glass was bent on-site, through a process called cold warping. The flat glass curtain wall panels were lifted into place, fixed to three points on the structure ("three points make a plane," as the saying goes) and then bent into their final position at the fourth corner. The result has been likened to a sailboat, appropriate given its location just steps from the Hudson River.

Continue to Eleventh Avenue and turn right, heading north past IAC headquarters and stopping at the north corner of 19th Street.

(I) 100 Eleventh Avenue
ATELIERS JEAN NOUVEL, 2010

The short walk past IAC reveals that, outside of a view into its lobby, Gehry's building offers little for the pedestrian on Eleventh Avenue. This is hardly surprising, given the avenue's car-centric nature, but Jean Nouvel's 23-story residential tower across 19th Street offers an alternative. At the corner, cut into the squared-off six-story base, pedestrians can access a ground-floor gallery space. This outdoor space was envisioned to be part of a restaurant in the tower's early days, but the noise of Eleventh Avenue makes the thought of outdoor seating perplexing. Look up within this outdoor space at the corner to see an unexpected presence: trees "floating" in metal-and-glass planters. Like Gehry, Nouvel's main expression is made with glass. Although the tower has a rounded corner facing southwest, all of the nearly 1,700 panels of glass facing south and west are flat. Like an abstract painting scaled up to building size, the façade is a composition of square and rectangular glazing of different sizes

set at different angles. Although apparently random, the glass and frames are actually part of large prefabricated modules that subtly describe a regular grid across the noisy façade.

Walk east along 19th Street and stop across the street from the loading dock serving Gehry's IAC Building.

(J)
Metal Shutter Houses
SHIGERU BAN ARCHITECTS, 2011 – 524 WEST 19TH STREET

Next door to Gehry's flamboyant mass of glass is its apparent antithesis: a regular grid of floors covered in what appears to be the metal roller gates that front so many New York City storefronts. Depending on how many people in the Metal Shutter Houses' nine condo units are home, some of the rolling shutters may be lifted, revealing glass walls behind the terraces. Even

(J)

with the shutters down, what lies behind can be grasped, due to the perforations allowing natural light and air as required by NYC building code. On rare occasions, the glass walls behind the shutters may be lifted, revealing duplex units with double-height living spaces. In his desire to provide houses rather than apartments, Japanese architect Shigeru Ban created something alien—dwellings that literally open themselves to the city.

Backtrack to Eleventh Avenue and then walk north to 20th Street, taking a right and stopping across the street from David Zwirner Gallery.

(K) David Zwirner Gallery

SELLDORF ARCHITECTS, 2013 – 537 WEST 20TH STREET

When the blocks in Chelsea alongside the High Line were rezoned in 2005, roughly five blocks were retained as manufacturing, in order to shift residential to other blocks and maintain the gallery uses that made the area a popular cultural destination. One of these blocks is the north side of 20th Street, where gallerist David Zwirner opened his second Chelsea gallery, a five-story building designed by Annabelle Selldorf. The exposed concrete façade— a rarity in NYC at the time—combines with the teak panels and window frames to give the building a decidedly Swiss appearance. The minimal detailing of the façade extends to the interior (worth a peek), where a dramatic concrete stair extends from the large, column-free gallery capped by sawtooth skylights on the ground floor to the smaller second-floor gallery and the private floors above. Zwirner's presence in Chelsea will expand with plans

(B3)

announced in 2018 for a five-story building on West 21st Street to be designed by Renzo Piano.

Continue east on 20th Street until you reach the High Line stairs near the end of the block. Head back up to the High Line and then turn right into Section 2 of the park. Pass through the dense thicket of trees and stop by the large seating area at 22nd Street.

(B3) 23rd Street Lawn, 2011

With a park made primarily of concrete and native plantings, this little patch of grass makes another special "moment." The only lawn on the High Line spans from 22nd Street to 23rd Street, "peeling up" much like the park's benches. Even more popular than the adjacent tiered seating made from stacked pieces of lumber, the lawn is often closed to recuperate after days of heavy use. Furthermore, the high edge of the lawn is rung with continuous seating and the small plaza beyond it regularly features artwork curated by the High Line.

(L) HL23

NEIL M. DENARI ARCHITECTS (NMDA), 2011 – 515 WEST 23RD STREET

NMDA's 14-story building for developer Alf Naman affords each of its eleven condos straight, not oblique, views up and down the High Line, a situation that arose from a spur widening the former railway at 23rd Street. About a fourth of the site's property sits beneath the High Line, so to recoup this lost area the building widens as it rises, until the roofline is the full 40-foot (12 m) width of the site. This cantilevered profile, enabled by variances to the zoning code, means the building wants to literally tumble onto the

High Line. Thankfully, diagonal steel bracing holds the structure in balance. Knowing that people living in glass boxes will need to pull their curtains every now and then, an image of the bracing is printed onto the glass walls facing south and north to make the structural forces perpetually visible. For further privacy, the east façade is primarily solid, with small windows amid sculpted stainless-steel panels.

Head north a few blocks, until the concrete planks give way to steel grating.

(B4) Woodland Flyover, 2011

The next "moment" spans two blocks, from 25th Street to 27th Street. Responding to a found "forest" in a narrow slot between industrial buildings on both sides of the High Line, the designers inserted an elevated walkway to create what is officially the Philip A. and Lisa Maria Falcone Flyover. The grated steel surface lifts park-goers up between stands of magnolia trees, while walkway extensions with benches invite people to sit among the trees. Breaking free of the park's kit of parts enables the soil to be mounded up high enough for the sizable trees and their root systems. At 26th Street is a small "viewing spur" with an illuminated frame that recalls the billboards that once attached themselves to the sides of the High Line.

Walk north and stop near 27th Street, the first street past the Flyover.

(M) 520 West 28th Street

ZAHA HADID ARCHITECTS, 2017

The signature flowing forms of Pritzker Prize–winning architect Zaha Hadid—one of four finalists in the park's 2004 competition—eventually sidled up next to the High Line with this 11-story condo development and its 39 units for Related Companies. Hadid, who died unexpectedly in March 2016, did not see the completion of her first NYC building. The L-shaped plan cradles some existing

buildings on 27th Street and abuts Brazilian architect Isay Weinfeld's relatively sedate Jardim condo development to the west. Hadid's curved lines are detailed with hand-rubbed metal profiles that frame the floor-to-ceiling glass walls and sizable projecting terraces. The metal folds weave together on the south and north façades to express the split levels of the plan's two legs. Though not visible to passersby, the flowing lines extend to the interiors that Hadid's firm also designed, resulting in an immersive environment for those fortunate—and rich—enough to snag one of the units.

Head north and stop at 29th Street, where the High Line starts to curve to the west.

(N) Soori High Line

SCDA, 2017 – 522 WEST 29TH STREET

Soo K. Chan, head of Singapore's SCDA Architects and Oriel Development, is responsible for two eleven-story condo buildings just west of the High Line, both facing each other across 29th Street. To the right is 515 West 29th Street with its rippling glass fins. Across the street on the south is the more fetching Soori High Line, whose elegant elevation facing the street is covered in vertical wood fins. The deep profile of the fins, and the privacy they ensure, is most notable from this oblique angle, as is the double-height living spaces behind the façade. To lure the super-rich, sixteen of the building's nearly thirty luxury units come with their own private lap pools.

(O) 10 Hudson Yards

KPF, 2016

Towering over us to the right—and a visual terminus in our northern walk along the High Line since at least 18th Street—is 10 Hudson Yards, the first tower completed in the massive Hudson Yards development. Once finished, Hudson Yards will consist of more than 18 million square feet (1.6 million sq m) in commercial and residential towers spread across 30 acres (12 ha) on platforms and air rights over active rail yards between Tenth Avenue and the West Side Highway, from 30th Street to 34th Street. The first phase, which covers four blocks east of Eleventh Avenue, is primarily office, while the second phase west of Eleventh Avenue will be mainly residential. KPF's 52-story office tower was built first due to its location at the southeast corner of Hudson Yards, where it sits at grade rather than over tracks. The glass tower with its angular silhouette notably overlaps the High Line—the first such building since The Standard [C]—where a spur crosses over Tenth Avenue, planned as a "piazza" for cultural programming.

How the Hudson Yards development came into being is too long and complex to recount in much detail here. Suffice it to say that two city administrations tried to deck over the rail yards that serve the Long Island Rail Road (LIRR): for Giuliani, it was the site of a proposed stadium for the Yankees, and for Bloomberg the rail yards were a major component in the city's 2012 Olympics bid. Although the latter failed, two separate rezonings for the area (one in 2004, a year before the High Line rezoning, and the other in 2009) opened the door for the current mixed-used development master-planned by KPF for Related with Oxford Properties Group.

Walk along the curved path lined with benches, cross 30th Street into Section 3 of the High Line, and ascend the steps to the plaza near the entrance to 10 Hudson Yards.

That Hudson Yards's platform closely aligns with the High Line three stories above the surrounding streets means the development exists uniquely as an extension of the linear park. This fact points to the creation of two special "somethings" between the numerous towers in the first phase, both nearing completion at the time of this writing.

(P) The Shed

DILLER SCOFIDIO+RENFO (DS+R) & ROCKWELL GROUP, 2019 –
15 HUDSON YARDS

First is the Shed, a cultural venue appended to the 70-story 15 Hudson Yards, both designed by DS+R and Rockwell Group. The tower starts as a rectangle but ends as a silhouette of

O
Q

bundled cylinders. Set into the tower at an angle are the Shed's translucent walls: lightweight, air-filled ETFE (ethylene tetrafluoroethylene) pillows that span up to 75 feet (22 m) at their corners. More impressive than the Shed's rippling skin is the fact that the whole eight-story-tall, steel-framed enclosure moves on rails and six-foot-diameter (1.8 m) "bogies" to transform the public outdoor space next to it into an enclosed space suitable for performances and other special events. Small motors mounted on the roof mean the movement is seen but not heard.

Q Vessel

HEATHERWICK STUDIO, 2019

Second is designer Thomas Heatherwick's *Vessel*, a huge piece of public art that sits at the center of the development's Public Square and Gardens designed by landscape architecture firm Nelson Byrd Woltz. Obviously inspired by the stepwells of India, Heatherwick fashioned 154 interconnecting flights of stairs, 2,400 steps, and 80 landings into a 150-foot-tall (46 m) accessible sculpture. The steel structure, which widens from 50 feet (15 m) at its base to 150 feet (45.7 m) at its apex, is covered on its underside with polished, copper-colored steel to reflect those traversing the sculpture.

> *Head back to the High Line, turn right and then*
> *stop just past the bridge over Eleventh Avenue.*

(B5) Pershing Square Beams, 2014

The Pershing Square Beams, as the sunken area west of Eleventh Avenue is called, is the only place on the whole 1.5-mile-long (2.4 km) High Line that approaches a playground. This kid-friendly area features a walkway depressed a couple of feet (60 cm) below the top of the existing beams, which were wrapped in a soft, protective layer. The designers entice and entertain small children with periscopes to peer through, small openings to crawl through, and a cage that pops up into one of the planting beds.

> *Continue past the playground and follow the curve of the*
> *High Line until reaching the seating area on the right made*
> *from large pieces of timber.*

(B6) Interim Walkway, 2014

Just a few paces past the Pershing Square Beams, the High Line changes character once again, its concrete planks giving way to asphalt and Piet Oudolf's curated plantings mixing with wildflowers and other self-sown plants. This interim section of the High Line, which slopes down gradually toward 34th Street, is the closest thing visitors come to experiencing the "found" park that took root after the railroad's closure in 1980 and that Joel Sternfeld dramatically captured in photos twenty years later. Often a setting for artworks, this area's otherwise continuous vegetation is split by tiered seating beside Twelfth Avenue,

a great spot to observe the ongoing construction of the Hudson Yards development.

Walk the remainder of the High Line and continue east along 34th Street, until reaching Hudson Boulevard E, between Tenth and Eleventh Avenues.

(R) Hudson Park and Boulevard

MICHAEL VAN VALKENBURGH ASSOCIATES, 2015

As early as 2004, when a large chunk of the West Side was rezoned for commercial and residential uses, a park was envisioned to work in concert with the 7 Line subway extension. The park is being realized in two phases: The first phase, running from the Hudson Yards Public Square and Gardens at 33rd Street up to 36th Street, was completed in 2015, while the second, northern phase to 39th Street is still in the planning phase. The three "islands" of green between the streets and new boulevards in the first phase have trees, benches, fountains, a playground, and a food and bathroom kiosk. It is a place of activity and respite rather than a place for strolling like the High Line. Also unlike the High Line, which is maintained and paid for primarily by the fund-raising efforts of the nonprofit FHL, Hudson Park and Boulevard is part of a BID (Business Improvement District) that levies a fee on commercial properties in the district to cover maintenance costs.

(S) 34 Street–Hudson Yards Subway Station

DATTNER ARCHITECTS, 2015

Projecting into the park on either side of 34th Street are glass canopies designed by architect Toshiko Mori for the 34 Street–Hudson Yards subway station, which opened in 2015. Dattner Architects designed everything below the canopies. Highlights of the station include the mosaic artworks by Xenobia Bailey and the superlong escalators and funicular that reach to the tracks below Eleventh Avenue. Although visitors to the High Line now reach the new subway station by walking along 34th Street, the dynamic will change greatly once the first phase of Hudson Yards is complete and the three public landscapes—the High Line, the Hudson Yards Public Square and Gardens, and Hudson Park and Boulevard— are united between Tenth and Eleventh Avenues. People will have less incentive to walk the section around the rail yards. But by that point, work will be advancing on the second phase of Hudson Yards, and the completion of the High Line's interim section.

End of tour is at the western terminus of the 7 Train, which is reached by the longest escalators in the New York City subway system.

4 Bowery Changing

⟩ *This tour starts at the intersection of Prince Street and the Bowery, in front of the New Museum of Contemporary Art, and ends at Astor Place, near the northern tip of the Bowery.*

In late 2001—a few months after the events of 9/11 and five years before moving to the city—my wife and I made our first trip to New York City as a couple, staying, of all places, on the Bowery. With plywood walls that stopped short of the ceiling, a bathroom down the narrow hall, and a room barely big enough for a twin bed and locker, calling the Whitehouse Hotel a *hotel* was a bit of a stretch. But at $50 a night the rooms were a bargain, and the lobby, where the backpackers and flophouse regulars mixed, made for a memorable stay. The Whitehouse opened in 1917 as one of the many flophouses along skid row, but in the 1990s its management sensed the changes and opened up some of its rooms for indiscriminate travelers like us. It closed in 2016—reportedly the last flophouse on the Bowery—nine years after The Bowery Hotel opened directly across the street, its 135 rooms starting around $400 per night. Sightings of panhandlers gave way to celebrity sightings. Added to the National Register of Historic Places in 2013, the Bowery of the twenty-first century is much different from that of the twentieth century—let alone earlier centuries.

Before the Bowery filled up with flophouses, Manhattan's oldest thoroughfare was an Indian trail that stretched up the east side of the island. It earned its name when the Dutch settled the island in the seventeenth century and used the trail to connect a series of farms, or *bouweries*. By then, the trail was shortened considerably—closer to its current length of 1.25 miles (2 km)—ending at the country estate of Peter Stuyvesant just north of present-day Cooper Square. Subsequently, the Bowery was widened to become a popular boulevard for houses of the rich and famous, followed by the construction of numerous pre-Broadway theaters. But as the population of New York City grew and development moved up the island, the houses and theaters moved north too. In their nineteenth-century wake came penny arcades, bars, brothels, and the first flophouses. The

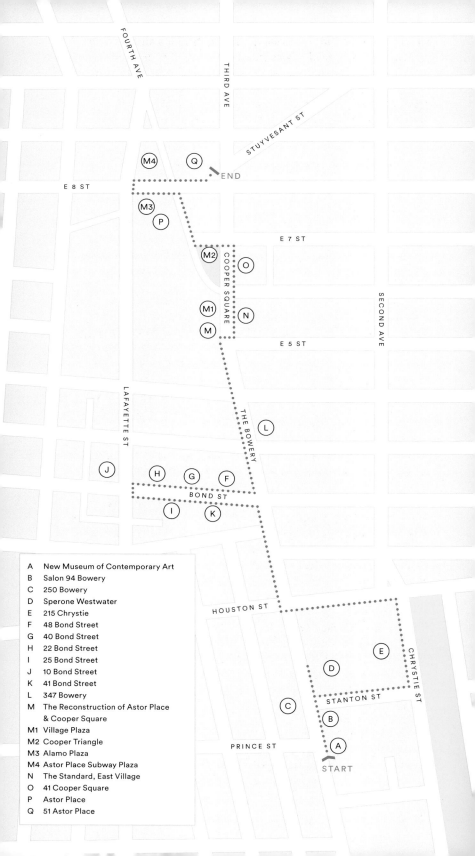

FOURTH AVE

THIRD AVE

STUYVESANT ST

M4 Q END

E 8 ST

M3
P

E 7 ST

M2 COOPER SQUARE O

SECOND AVE

M1 N

M E 5 ST

THE BOWERY

L

LAFAYETTE ST

J H G F

BOND ST

I K

HOUSTON ST

E CHRYSTIE ST

D

C STANTON ST

B

PRINCE ST A

START

A   New Museum of Contemporary Art
B   Salon 94 Bowery
C   250 Bowery
D   Sperone Westwater
E   215 Chrystie
F   48 Bond Street
G   40 Bond Street
H   22 Bond Street
I   25 Bond Street
J   10 Bond Street
K   41 Bond Street
L   347 Bowery
M   The Reconstruction of Astor Place
    & Cooper Square
M1 Village Plaza
M2 Cooper Triangle
M3 Alamo Plaza
M4 Astor Place Subway Plaza
N   The Standard, East Village
O   41 Cooper Square
P   Astor Place
Q   51 Astor Place

presence of the Third Avenue El casting its noise and shadow on the streets and sidewalks from 1878 to 1955 cemented this downward trend and earned the Bowery its skid row label. Then, starting in the 1970s, the city dispersed its homeless population beyond the Bowery, leading to the closure of flophouses and shelters; of the latter, only the Bowery Mission remains—two doors down from the first stop on this tour.

New Museum of Contemporary Art

SANAA, 2007 – 235 BOWERY

The Bowery starts at Chatham Square in Chinatown, about a half mile (0.8 km) south of here. The most dramatic changes to the thoroughfare have taken place north of Chinatown, in the stretches bordering the Lower East Side, Nolita, NoHo, and the East Village. Today's changes began with the New Museum of Contemporary Art, which bought a parcel on the Bowery in 2002 and announced its relocation from SoHo to the Bowery. The move made sense for the New Museum, which was founded in 1977 and moved to the Astor Building at 583 Broadway in 1983, around the peak of SoHo's art scene. By then, some of the artists who made SoHo a popular postindustrial area had moved to the Bowery; the New Museum followed suit just a few decades later, eschewing the Chelsea lofts where many galleries went in favor of a former parking lot that could give the institution a strong identity through a new building.

That identity came from SANAA, the Japanese firm of architects Kazuyo Sejima and Ryue Nishizawa, who won an international competition for the commission in 2003. The design—seven stacked boxes, each one shifted slightly from the next to insert skylights into the windowless galleries—fits the 175-foot-tall (53 m) building within its zoning envelope, and gives the New Museum its singular identity. (The success of the last is visible in the museum's logo, an outline of the building when seen from the Bowery.) The height of the boxes corresponds to their contents: the transparent lobby and loading dock at sidewalk level; offices in the shallow second box; three levels of galleries above; an education center in the sixth box; and an event space at the top, where a terrace opens to expansive views over the low-scale surroundings. White walls, concrete floors, and exposed ceilings frame the contemporary art inside, while expanded aluminum mesh over corrugated aluminum panels covers the whole exterior, giving the building a rough-but-sexy appearance that befits its location on the Bowery and at the start of Prince Street.

How well SANAA's bold design holds up as an architectural statement will depend upon the actions of Rem Koolhaas and Shohei Shigematsu of OMA, who were selected by the museum in late 2017 (over SANAA and a few others) to design an expansion

at 231 Bowery, between the SANAA building and the Bowery
Mission. The new 50,000-square-foot (4,645 sq m) building
will roughly double the museum's square footage, and add a
high-profile sibling of contemporary architecture to the Bowery,
something unthinkable decades before.

Walk up the Bowery a few steps.

B Salon 94 Bowery
RAFAEL VIÑOLY ARCHITECTS, 2011 – 243 BOWERY

A video screen and glass door at the base of a five-story brick
building signal the two-room gallery of Salon 94's third location.
Head inside to see the small lobby behind the video screen and
a large white-cube gallery in the cellar, where a skylight illuminates
the back wall (reminiscent of the New Museum galleries). Most
appealing is the straight stair connecting the two rooms, where
two details stand out: an exposed steel beam mounted to the
ceiling that extends from the entrance to the middle of the gallery
space, and an über-minimal handrail seamlessly cut into one
wall of the stair. The former aids in bringing large artworks in and
out of the space, while the latter does the same for art lovers.

C 250 Bowery
MORRIS ADJMI ARCHITECTS & AA STUDIO, 2013

What made SoHo more amenable to artists' studios and galleries
was the building stock: sturdy, iron-framed industrial lofts with
open plans. The Bowery did not have that, meaning the arrival of
the art scene took longer and was thinner than in neighborhoods
like Chelsea and Bushwick, Brooklyn, that took over SoHo's role
after it proved too costly. Nevertheless, architects Morris Adjmi
and Aldo Andreoli designed their own version of a loft building
for the Bowery, with 24 condo units for VE Equities behind a grid
of factory sash windows, its steel structure expressed through
metal channels. The out-of-place building is also home for the
International Center of Photography, located in a space designed
by Skidmore, Owings & Merrill (SOM).

Walk up the Bowery one block.

D Sperone Westwater
FOSTER + PARTNERS, 2010 – 257 BOWERY

Sperone Westwater celebrated 35 years of dealing art when it
moved from the Meatpacking District to this narrow, eight-story
building on the Bowery. Norman Foster's design features dark-
metal sidewalls and a translucent glass façade, the latter veiling

a bright red box. The box might be on the second floor one week, the fourth floor the next; although it is a room, an extension of the galleries inside, it is also an elevator, movable based on the whims of the gallery and what it displays inside. Walking into the lobby of Sperone Westwater, with the rails on the side leading the eye up to the elevator overhead, can be a jarring experience—standing in an elevator shaft, even a quasi one like this, doesn't happen every day. Visit the gallery when the room/elevator is located at the fifth floor and the shaft is tall, voluminous; but if it's at the lowest position, on the second floor, the feeling is compressed, borderline claustrophobic. Beyond the glass, concrete, and metal walls of the lobby/shaft are fairly typical gallery spaces with white walls and ceilings and polished concrete floors. Take the elevator, located past the double-height gallery on the first floor, to access the upstairs galleries (1 through 3 are public, 4 and 5 are private, and the top three floors serve as offices and library), and see where the gallery extension is parked. Although the interior of the movable room is yet another white cube for art, its presence on the Bowery, especially at night, is undeniable.

*Walk south and turn left at Stanton Street, head east and
turn left at Chrystie Street.*

(E) **215 Chrystie**

HERZOG & DE MEURON, 2017

The first collaboration between hotelier Ian Schrager and architects Jacques Herzog and Pierre de Meuron (40 Bond Street, [G]) saw Schrager venture into new territory: condos. The team reunited about a decade later for two new projects: condos on Leroy Street [2L] and this Lower East Side building that combines hotel and condos into one. At the base of the 28-story building is the 367-room Public hotel and above it, in a setback tower, are 11 half- and full-floor condos. Uniting them is the external concrete frame—its wood-grain finish is visible on the lower floors—with inclined columns and floor-to-ceiling glass walls. The differences between the base and top are slight but noticeable: the hotel has twice as many columns, windows that follow the inclined columns, and solid corners where the opposing inclines meld together; with fewer columns, the condos' exterior window walls are more expansive, tucked vertically into the concrete slabs, and fully glazed at the corners.

Set back from Chrystie Street and fronted by a manicured landscape accessed by concrete portals, the mid-block building looks like a corner building, thanks to the parking lot of neighboring 10 Stanton Street. That housing complex, which wraps around from the Bowery, was given a twenty-five-year extension on its 147 affordable units as part of the sale of the previously vacant lot to Schrager. Although low-income housing and multimillion dollar condos are strange bedfellows, they're not as dramatic a change as the "luxury for all" Public, with its snazzy escalators (worth a look) leading to the second-floor lobby, and its two restaurants, three lounges, and performance space.

Walk up to Houston Street, turn left and walk to the west corner of Bowery; turn right and walk up to the Belgian block Bond Street, home to a handful of condo developments from this century. Walk about halfway down the south side of the block to look at buildings across the street.

(F) ## 48 Bond Street

DEBORAH BERKE & PARTNERS, 2008

The angled planes projecting from the otherwise flat granite and glass façade look like operable windows at first glance, but they are fixed, an effort to enliven the building with shadows over the course of the day. Designed for developer Romy Goldman, the 11-story building designed by Deborah Berke has 16 apartments, with the top few floors set back from the façade that lines up with its older neighbors.

G 40 Bond Street

HERZOG & DE MEURON, 2007

The development that made this stretch of Bond Street once again popular for living (row houses and mansions covered the street into the mid-1800s) is the first collaboration of hotelier Ian Schrager and Swiss architects Jacques Herzog and Pierre de Meuron. The ten-story building was completed one year before the NoHo Historic District Extension, which encompasses most of this block. But since the design pays homage to industrial lofts, cast iron architecture, and the area's twentieth-century art scene, it probably would have been approved easily by the Landmarks Preservation Commission (LPC). Whatever the case, the curved green glass (layered with stainless-steel reflectors) covering the concrete frame at the level of the apartments combine with the "graffiti gates" (made from cast aluminum and worth a touch) at the townhouses to form one of the most memorable apartment buildings in Manhattan this century. A few invisible details: the undulating lobby is so narrow, and the building lacks a loading dock, so large pieces of furniture are moved in and out of the apartments via cherry pickers and windows that swing open; on the rear elevation, blackened copper echoes the curved glass on the front; and Schrager appreciates the building so much he lives in an 11th-floor penthouse added to the top of the building in 2009 by John Pawson.

Walk west along the south side of the street to 25 Bond Street.

(H) 22 Bond Street
BKSK ARCHITECTS, 2019

The financial crisis left the 14-story concrete structure of a
planned hotel an empty shell waiting for façades and interior
finishes that never arrived. Richport Group and SDS Brooklyn
took over the project, lopped off three floors (in response to
a historic district created in the interim), and brought in BKSK
to turn it into residential lofts. Faced with a Bond Street address
but a building set back to Great Jones Street, the architects
created a Cor-Ten steel front wall and a private "art garden"
that can be glimpsed through perforations. The project's Bond
Street presence isn't all urban rust: a window at sidewalk level
was designed to frame a sculpture by NoHo artist Roy Nachum.

(I) 25 Bond Street
BKSK ARCHITECTS, 2007

About ten years before BKSK reworked 22 Bond, the firm designed
this eight-story condo development for Goldman Properties.
Typical for the developer, but not others, seven of the nine
"dream homes" were sold to partners on the project, making the
development more bespoke than speculative, more townhouse
than condo. Architecturally, the limestone façade layered in front
of sliding glass walls grabs the most attention, though look down
for something unexpected: granite sidewalk blocks carved by
artist Kenichi Hiratsuka hold their own with Bond Street's paving.

Continue west to Lafayette Street.

(J) 10 Bond Street
SELLDORF ARCHITECTS, 2015

Although this corner lot is situated in the NoHo Historic District,
designated in 1999, for more than seventy-five years it was
home to gas stations and auto repair shops—hardly uses worth
protection. But when Annabelle Selldorf was hired by a trio of
developers to design a seven-story building with eleven residences
(a townhouse, nine apartments, and a penthouse), LPC still had
a say in its design. Selldorf was more than capable, developing
curved terracotta panels with a rust-orange glaze between
large windows and Cor-Ten details at the storefront and roof.
The building's oddest feature—the rooftop pergola shading the
penthouse's wraparound terrace—was added in response to LPC
concerns that the building was too low relative to its neighbors.

Cross Bond Street and walk east along the north side
of the street to 40 Bond Street to look across the street.

99

41 Bond Street
DDG, 2011

In 2007, developer Adam Gordon bought a few parcels on this stretch of Bond Street: the cast-iron Bouwerie Lane Theatre from 1874, which he renovated into three huge residences, and 41–43 Bond Street, planned as an eight-story building with eight units. For the latter, he hired architects Steven Harris to design a building that required LPC approval. He got it—just in time for the economy to tank. Luckily in 2009 he found a buyer in DDG, a new design, development, and construction company that would use 41 Bond Street to prove themselves. Starting with the "bones" of Harris's approved design—limestone façade with planter boxes and a regular grid of windows with shutters—DDG retained most features but changed the details. Most dramatic is the handcrafted bluestone in narrow slabs, a material the firm has used repeatedly since. The shutters are gone, but plants remain, sprouting from bluestone planters to cover more of the façade each year.

*Return to the Bowery, turn left and walk north
to East 3rd Street.*

 ## 347 Bowery
SELLDORF ARCHITECTS, 2017

From the corner balconies climbing the setback tower above the two-story base, it's clear where the views are: Lower Manhattan. Taking the place of the Salvation Army's East Village Residence, which closed in 2008, the 13-story building comprises only five residential units in the tower: four duplex townhouses and a triplex penthouse. Custom bricks from Denmark clad the base, while zinc is used on the tower. The simple building is a welcome presence on the Bowery, especially from the southwest, where it blocks the tall but architecturally inferior tower designed by Robert Scarano Jr.

*Walk up the Bowery to East 5th Street and
cross to the west side of the Bowery.*

 ## The Reconstruction of Astor Place & Cooper Square
WXY, 2016

In May 2009, stretches of Broadway, where it intersected with Times Square and Herald and Greeley Squares, were closed to cars. This pedestrianization of automobile space was part of a larger plan spearheaded by Mayor Bloomberg's Department of Transportation commissioner Janette Sadik-Khan and based on the research and design work of urban designer Jan Gehl from Copenhagen. Gehl's plan for increasing public space focused on Broadway and extended as far south as Astor Place and Cooper Square, even though these spaces are one block east of the diagonal thoroughfare. Two years after those closures, the city unveiled plans by WXY and Quennell Rothschild & Partners for stitching together a series of old and new plazas oriented about Astor Place and Cooper Square, from East 4th Street north to East 9th Street. Their design is focused around four spaces, from south to north: Village Plaza, Cooper Triangle, Alamo Plaza, and Astor Place Subway Plaza.

(M1) Village Plaza

North of East 4th Street the Bowery branches off into two avenues: Third Avenue on the east and Fourth Avenue on the west, with the junction up to East 8th Street known as Cooper Square. With only slivers of medians between the lanes of traffic, crossing Cooper Square was confusing and oftentimes a gamble. But as part of the reconstruction, two lanes of traffic were removed and Fourth Avenue was rerouted. In their place is the sunny Village Plaza, a block-long triangular space with seating, plantings, and a feeling of safety where there wasn't before.

(N)

(N) The Standard, East Village

CARLOS ZAPATA STUDIO, 2009 – 25 COOPER SQUARE

When the billowing 21-story Cooper Square Hotel across the Bowery opened in 2009, it was such a huge jump in scale from its neighbors that many critics saw it as a middle finger to the Bowery and the East Village. Since then much has changed: the low brick building to the north was demolished to make way for the blocky, 12-story dormitory at the corner; the hotel was sold to André Balazs in 2011 and became the second Standard in Manhattan (it accompanies the Standard, High Line [3C]); the hotel expanded into the former tenement building to the south, which now serves as the main entrance; and brick and wooden storefronts were pasted onto Carlos Zapata's milky white-glass tower, continuing the traditional language of the renovated neighbor.

Cross to the east side of the Bowery to see hotel up close, then walk north up Cooper Square one block.

(O) 41 Cooper Square

MORPHOSIS, 2009

If there has been one steady element along the Bowery for the last century and a half, it is the Cooper Union, founded by industrialist and inventor Peter Cooper as the Cooper Union for the Advancement of Science and Art in 1859. The landmark Foundation Building, designed by Frederick A. Petersen, was completed the same year as one of the first structures built with

rolled iron beams and designed to accommodate an elevator. More than this stately home, Cooper Union was known for its tuition-free scholarships ("free as water and air" in Cooper's words), enabled primarily by the school's ownership of the land under the Chrysler Building and investments. But ongoing financial strain led the school to charge its roughly 900 students tuition—from free to more than $20,000 per semester—starting in 2014. Critics, many of them former students, immediately pointed to 41 Cooper Square, the more than $100 million building designed by California's Thom Mayne, as the culprit. Though expensive, the new building was actually part of Cooper Union's attempt to rein in its finances: it moved its engineering department from the block north of the Foundation Building to 41 Cooper Square, leasing that block for the new 51 Astor Place office building [Q].

Marking Cooper Union's 150th anniversary, 41 Cooper Square boldly takes the school in a daring formal direction, one that props itself up on diagonal concrete columns and expresses the building's inner logic behind a perforated stainless-steel veil. Morphosis arranged the classrooms, studios, and other spaces for the departments of engineering, humanities, and the arts (architecture is in the Foundation Building) around what Mayne calls "a vertical piazza," a complex series of stairs meant to foster interaction among students. The main stair ascends diagonally—and dramatically—from the corner lobby for four floors, after which more asymmetrical stairs are stacked to the ninth floor. This path is expressed in part on the elevation facing Cooper Square as angular cuts in the metal skin, a skin that juts away from the glass box beneath it toward the corner entrance.

Glance up at the sizable cavity between the metal skin and glass wall at the corner entry, then cross Cooper Square to get a better look at the building.

(M2) Cooper Triangle

The most sizable existing portion of the public spaces at Astor Place and Cooper Square was Peter Cooper Park, which was given to the city by descendants of Peter Stuyvesant but then renamed in honor of Cooper Union's founder in 1883. Even though all but one of the mature trees have been retained, the gated park now known as Cooper Triangle benefits from two more access points, larger plantings, and a strong buffer along Fourth Avenue, where two lanes were removed. A bronze statue of Cooper from 1894 still presides over the park.

Walk up Fourth Avenue to East 8th Street and head west across Fourth Avenue.

(M3) Alamo Plaza

With the honor of being the first permanent contemporary
outdoor sculpture installed in NYC, in 1967, Tony Rosenthal's
Alamo was an immensely popular piece that required crossing
four lanes of traffic to reach on its own trapezoidal island.
Once there, people touching the painted Cor-Ten steel cube
would discover it could spin easily atop its base. The sculpture
underwent minor restorations in 2005 but was removed again
during the Reconstruction of Astor Place and Cooper Square,
when it received a more substantial restoration. Its welcome
reinstallation in November 2016 marked the Reconstruction's
completion and a new name for the larger plaza.

(P) Astor Place

GWATHMEY SIEGEL & ASSOCIATES, 2006 – 445 LAFAYETTE STREET

Before Cooper Union leased 51 Astor Place for ninety-nine
years to pay for 41 Cooper Square, the college tried a similar
maneuver for the prominent site across from its Foundation
Building, long a parking lot. The first attempt, a pre-40 Bond [G]
collaboration between Ian Schrager and Herzog & de Meuron
with Rem Koolhaas for a boutique hotel, didn't take. In stepped
Related Companies, coming off of Time Warner Center [6B],
which hired Charles Gwathmey to design a residential tower
above a retail podium. It's hard to find many kind words about
the undulating glass-walled building (Paul Goldberger's review
at the time was titled "Green Monster"), which was marketed
under the slogan "Sculpture for Living"—now it is more fitting as
a backdrop for *Alamo* than as anything sculptural in its own right.

Head north across East 8th Street.

(M4) Astor Place Subway Plaza

The northernmost section of the Reconstruction of Astor Place
and Cooper Square is oriented about the reconstructed subway
canopy leading to the 1904 Interborough Rapid Transit Company
(IRT) station. New features, such as plantings and WXY's Zipper
benches, keep their distance from the subway entrance. Much of
the seating is oriented toward Fumihiko Maki's new office building
across Fourth Avenue rather than Daniel Burnham's Wanamaker
department store across Lafayette Street; the former's dark-glass
façade does skillfully reflect the latter though.

(Q) 51 Astor Place

MAKI AND ASSOCIATES, 2013

As noted already, the land beneath this 14-story speculative office building is owned by Cooper Union, leased to Edward J. Minskoff Equities for ninety-nine years. The small block was previously home to the college's six-story Engineering Building, an unexceptional modern brick building with a low-slung coffee shop addition by Smith-Miller + Hawkinson at the southeast corner. Maki's building is architecturally superior, but it is imposing, particularly when seen from the Astor Place Subway Plaza, and out of place, more akin to the area around the architect's own 4 World Trade Center [1P] than the brick-and-stone East Village context.

*Cross Fourth Avenue and walk east on East 8th Street
to 51 Astor Place's plaza.*

A walk along the building's southern edge reveals the geometric complexity of its massing: what looks like a rectangular slab from the west is a slender parallelogram combined with a shorter trapezoid and a much shorter, five-side polygon. The last, instead of filling this southeast corner of the site, is cut along the angle of Stuyvesant Street to the east, in the process creating a plaza (by landscape architect Thomas Balsley) and preserving a view of the street that once formed the entrance to Peter Stuyvesant's *bouwerie*.

End of tour. Walk a couple of blocks east along Stuyvesant Street to see St. Mark's Church-in-the-Bowery, where Peter Stuyvesant is buried. Or walk one block west to access the subway, at [M4].

5

57th Street
River to River

⟩ *This tour starts at Sutton Place Park, at the eastern end
of 57th Street overlooking the East River, and ends
at Twelfth Avenue, just steps from the Hudson River.*

Although this tour traverses the entire two-mile (3.2 km) length
of 57th Street, from the East River to the Hudson River, the walk
is centered around the blocks between Park Avenue and Eighth
Avenue near Central Park, where a handful of residential supertalls
(skyscrapers exceeding 1,000 feet [300 m]) have made their mark
on the Midtown skyline. While the tour focuses on this recent
phenomenon of skinny towers for the superrich, walking the whole
length of 57th Street puts these projects into a wider context,
capturing the wide thoroughfare's many differences while moving
people beyond the well-traversed avenues in the island's center.
Before heading off, it's imperative to define a few terms—legal
mechanisms that affect buildings in the rest of the city but have
converged here to create "Billionaires' Row."

Floor Area Ratio (FAR): The ratio of a building's total floor area
(excluding such features as elevators, mechanical shafts, and
balconies) to lot size. FAR was introduced in New York City's 1961
Zoning Resolution, the first significant update since the original
resolution in 1916. A lot's FAR, which varies depending upon its
zoning district, determines the maximum floor area that can be
built upon it, with variation arising from lot coverage. For example,
a project on a zoning lot with an FAR of 10 could be 10 stories if it
fills the whole lot, 20 stories if it fills only half, 40 stories if it fills
a quarter, and so on, as long as the resulting square footage does
not exceed 10 times the lot area.

A couple of means allow developers to build more than the
zoning allows. First is *Privately Owned Public Spaces (POPS)*:
plazas, arcades, and other spaces primarily in dense commercial
districts that a developer/owner provides and subsequently
maintains in exchange for a bump in FAR. Per a New York City
Comptroller audit in April 2017, POPS are found in 333 locations
in the city, many in Midtown. Inserted into the city's zoning law
at the same time as FAR, the two mechanisms worked together

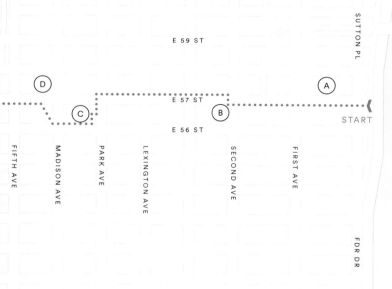

E 59 ST

SUTTON PL

D

C

E 57 ST

A

B

START

E 56 ST

FIFTH AVE

MADISON AVE

PARK AVE

LEXINGTON AVE

SECOND AVE

FIRST AVE

EAST RIVER

FDR DR

A   441 East 57th Street
B   Aalto 57
C   432 Park Avenue
D   LVMH
E   111 West 57th Street
F   One57
G   Central Park Tower
H   220 Central Park South
I   Hearst Tower
J   VIA 57 West

in the 1960s, 70s, and 80s, when most POPS were created, to shift tall buildings in Manhattan from "wedding cake" profiles to simple boxes.

Second is *Air Rights* (or unused development rights): the difference between a lot's maximum floor area and its actual floor area. There are two common methods for either purchasing air rights or combining multiple lots into a larger single lot, respectively: carrying out a *Transfer of Development Rights (TDR)*, or negotiating for a *Zoning Lot Merger (ZLM)*. TDRs allow building owners to sell any unused air rights to the owner of an adjacent or nearby property. Most of the TDRs along Billionaires' Row involve designated landmarks, buildings that cannot easily be torn down or built upon. ZLMs, on the other hand, combine contiguous lots within a block into a larger, merged lot, over which the FAR can be distributed as desired—into, in some cases, skinny supertalls. ZLMs are created through private transactions that are free from city approvals, one reason they have supplanted POPS as the most popular means of building taller.

The supertalls clustered along 57th Street can be seen as the latest phase in the evolution of the city's residential architecture, beginning with townhouses from the early-to-mid-1800s, apartment buildings that blossomed in the late 1800s and early 1900s, and towers that took advantage of the extra FAR that POPS afforded. Examples of early phases are evident here: in the late nineteenth-century townhouses to the north of Sutton Place Park and the One Sutton Place apartment building to the south, designed by Rosario Candela and completed in 1925. Both back up against gardens that cascaded down to the East River—until the construction of FDR Drive in the 1930s, that is. The small brick-paved park you're standing in was created at the time, compensation for creating a fissure between the streets of the primarily residential Sutton Place neighborhood and the waterfront below.

Walk out of the park along the south side of 57th Street, cross Sutton Place, and stop opposite 441 East 57th Street.

 ## 441 East 57th Street

FLANK, 2009

This slender glass-and-steel building appears to respect its neighbor to the east, 447 East 57th Street (another Candela building from the 1920s), through the breathing room it provides the older building. But residents of the Candela building, most notably former *Vogue* editor Tina Brown, sued to stop the project developed and designed by Flank, which involved the demolition of an old townhouse next to their side garden. Obviously they lost the lawsuit, and six units ranging in size from 1,700 to 5,500 square

feet (158–511 m) across 15 floors were erected on the townhouse lot. Each unit has a different layout, interlocking with the units above and/or below, expressed through dark reveals cut into the glass façade. This complex interplay extends to the 1,500 glass panes that fit together like a puzzle, some of them treated with frit patterns that recall Pierre Chareau's Maison de Verre in Paris.

Continue west along 57th Street until Second Avenue,
then cross to the intersection's northeast corner.

B Aalto 57

SKIDMORE, OWINGS & MERRILL (SOM), 2017 – 1065 SECOND AVENUE

The name of the project formerly known simply as 252 East 57th Street acknowledges an influence on SOM's Roger Duffy: the great Finnish architect Alvar Aalto. Specifically, the 65-story tower's undulating glass walls—inverted bay windows that widen toward the 700-foot-tall (213 m) top—recall the famous glass vase designed by Alvar and his wife Aino in the 1930s. The elegant tower, which places condos above rental units, is part of a larger project for developers World Wide Group and Rose Associates that includes two schools—P.S. 59 Beekman Hill International School and High School of Art and Design—and retail. The latter are housed in an adjacent structure that was also designed by SOM but looks distinctly different: stacked boxes with dark glass and dark-and-light metal panels. The schools previously sat on the site of the tower, so the new schools and retail were built first and then the old schools were demolished to make way for the residential tower.

> *Cross Second Avenue and continue west along 57th Street,*
> *stopping at Third Avenue.*

A good view of 432 Park Avenue, which is discussed in detail soon, is afforded at this corner. Worth noting from this vantage point are the two-story openings that occur roughly every dozen floors. These openings coincide with mechanical floors and outrigger trusses tying the exterior frame to the central core; they reduce the wind forces acting upon the tower; they elevate the residential units higher than they'd be without these non-FAR floors; and they glow after sunset.

> *Continue west on 57th Street and cross to the southwest corner*
> *of Park Avenue, then walk south to the portal on the right.*

Take a quick glance across Park Avenue at 425 Park Avenue, an office tower under construction at the time of writing. Norman Foster won an invited competition in 2012 (besting fellow heavyweights Zaha Hadid, Rem Koolhaas, and Richard Rogers) with a stepped form that recalls post-1916 "wedding cake" buildings but is highlighted by dramatic diagonal bracing at each successive setback. This form is not accidental; the new tower retains part of the old building to use the predecessor's pre-1961 zoning rules, which allow for more floor area but also dictate a stepped massing.

> *Walk through the portal to the small plaza.*

432 Park Avenue
RAFAEL VIÑOLY ARCHITECTS, 2015

Like SOM's Aalto 57, Rafael Viñoly's proudly geometric design for developer Harry Macklowe finds its inspiration in industrial design: a trash can designed by Austrian architect Josef Hoffmann last century. But translating a metal can with square openings to a 1,396-foot-tall (425 m) building with 10-foot-square (3 m) windows is no easy feat. And with such a slender profile—calculated at a width-to-height ratio of 1:15—this source of inspiration is an interesting tidbit but easily forgotten when confronted with the unrelenting grid of concrete and glass.

   The tower's attention-getting height and slenderness is enabled by a number of things working together: the openings at the mechanical floors, mentioned earlier; a tuned mass damper at the top of the building that counteracts strong winds; the provision of only six elevators in the compact core; a combination of TDRs, ZLMs, and POPS for extra floors; and tall floor-to-floor heights of 15 feet 6 inches (4.75 m). This height enables the scissor stairs—common in just about all New York City towers—in the core to work as highly compact, intertwining switchback stairs rather than

straight stairs that would eat into salable floor area. Skyscraper Museum founder Carol Willis includes this height in what she calls "The Logic of Luxury," the characteristics of slender supertalls.

432 Park Avenue is a rare skyscraper, for NYC at least, that combines structure and surface in one: the exterior's concrete columns and beams are exposed to the elements. Looking up at the tower reveals a consistent width to each column, but their depth tapers as the tower ascends, from more than 5 feet (1.5 m) at the base to 18 inches (46 cm) at the penthouse, which sold for nearly $100 million in 2013. Also at the base are four other pieces of 432 Park Avenue: four floors of offices on 57th Street, subterranean retail accessed by escalators at the Park Avenue portal, a retail "cube" on the corner of 56th Street and Park Avenue, and a POPS plaza. Finally, if the plaza's marble paving, grid of trees, and movable tables and chairs recall the famous Paley Park on East 53rd Street near Fifth Avenue, that's no accident; both plazas were designed by Zion Breen Richardson Associates. The new plaza may not be as memorable as its predecessor from 1967, but it's refreshing to find a public amenity accompanying 57th Street's luxury housing.

Walk west on 56th Street and enter the atrium of
590 Madison Avenue.

Bamboo fills the glass-topped atrium that Edward Larrabee Barnes designed as part of the IBM Building from 1983. It is one of the most successful POPS in the city, in contrast to two contemporaneous POPS a stone's throw away: to the south is the former AT&T Building's plaza by Philip Johnson, later maligned by Charles Gwathmey when Sony bought the building (as of this writing the plaza may be opened up to the elements and made larger and more green under a new owner); and to the west is direct access to Trump Tower, which was designed by Der Scutt with a whopping four POPS: a corridor and lobby on the ground floor and two hard-to-find roof terraces up a few floors. Through the corridor and the security detail is the atrium where Donald J. Trump announced his presidential candidacy and, in the cellar, some of the nicest publicly accessible restrooms in Midtown Manhattan.

Continue diagonally through the atrium to 57th Street and stop on the sidewalk.

(D) LVMH
CHRISTIAN DE PORTZAMPARC, 1999 – 19 EAST 57TH STREET

New York City architecture was in a bit of a lull in the 1990s, due in great part to a recession in the decade's first half as well as a lack of stylistic direction after the waning years of Postmodernism. Portzamparc's folded LVMH was a breath of fresh air when it was completed just shy of the millennium. Housing the North American headquarters of Moët Hennessy Louis Vuitton group, the 24-story building is logically located just steps from the luxury thoroughfare of Fifth Avenue. A Dior shop occupies the storefront space, but the appealing parts are upstairs, where the curtain wall—some panes etched to frame trapezoidal vision glass—is faceted and folded to give the tower's otherwise conventional stepped mass an asymmetrical gemlike appearance.

Walk west along the south side of 57th Street, crossing Fifth Avenue and stopping just shy of Sixth Avenue.

(E) 111 West 57th Street
SHOP ARCHITECTS, 2019

Of the supertalls going up along Billionaires' Row, 111 West 57th Street may not be the tallest, but it is easily the skinniest. At nearly 60 feet (18 m) wide and 1,428 feet (435 m) tall, the 82-story tower has a slenderness ratio of approximately 1:24. Although that number garners the most attention, the project's "vanity height"— the difference between the architectural top and the highest occupied floor—is also great: nearly 300 feet (91 m), given the highest of its 58 condo units sits at 1,134 feet (345 m). The space in between houses an 800-ton (725 tonnes) tuned mass damper, which works with the substantial shear walls on the east and west sides and outrigger walls at the mechanical floors to stabilize the building from lateral forces. The most striking architectural feature is the "feathered" profile that sets back from 57th Street and gives the east and west façades their expression: thin bands of terracotta panels with curved profiles alternate with slender windows and bronze frames. SHoP Architects and their frequent client JDS Development Group (here with Property Markets Group) managed such a slender supertall—on the same block as One57 [F], no less—by starting the condos at the 20th floor, above the neighboring buildings; providing tall floor-to-floor heights, à la 432 Park Avenue, and gaining air rights from the landmarked Steinway Hall incorporated into the project.

(F) One57

CHRISTIAN DE PORTZAMPARC, 2014 – 157 WEST 57TH STREET

Only six buildings separate 111 West 57th Street from the first Billionaires' Row supertall: One57. Hired in 2005 by Extell Development, Christian de Portzamparc was initially slated with designing several towers on the site, but after fifteen years of TDRs and ZLMs the project congealed into a single tower 1,004

(F)

feet (306 m) tall. The 75-story tower houses 132 condos as well as the 210-room Park Hyatt hotel. Marked by an angled, curved apex and smaller curves at each setback, the glass tower is covered in blue pinstripes that give it a dated, postmodern appearance. More than any architectural merits, One57 is known for record-setting sales—the $100 million penthouse in 2012—and the crane collapse televised around the world during Hurricane Sandy that same year.

> *Continue west along the south side of 57th Street and*
> *stop at the light across from One57.*

After craning your neck to see the top of One57, glance down to read the sign on the stoplight: 6 1/2 Avenue. This oddity is not just a pedestrian crosswalk across busy 57th Street: it is the endpoint of what's also known as Holly Whyte Way, a network of thru-block POPS and pedestrian-right-of-way crossings that reach all the way down to 51st Street.

> *Walk west once again along the south side of 57th Street,*
> *cross Seventh Avenue and stop halfway down the block.*

(G) Central Park Tower

ADRIAN SMITH + GORDON GILL ARCHITECTURE (AS+GG), 2020 –
217 WEST 57TH STREET

Through a series of TDRs and ZLMs, Extell—applying lessons learned from One57—combined the air rights from all but two lots on this block spanning from Seventh Avenue to Broadway. The result will be the tallest residential building in the United States—displacing 432 Park Avenue from that top spot. At 1,550 feet (472 m), Central Park Tower will be the second-tallest building in New York City, behind only One World Trade Center (1WTC) [1S]. A planned spire would have bumped the tower's height to 1,775 feet (541 m), one foot short of 1WTC, but it was dropped in 2015; nevertheless, the 1,550-foot-high (472 m) roof height is taller than the roof of 1WTC. For Chicago's AS+GG, this supertall is relatively short, since the partners are responsible for two megatalls (skyscrapers exceeding 2,000 feet [600 m]): the Burj Khalifa (2,722 feet [830 m]) and Jeddah Tower (3,281 feet [1000 m]).

   The base of Central Park Tower will contain New York City's first Nordstrom department store, but the most dramatic feature is the 28-foot-deep (8 m) cantilever that starts 200 feet (61 m) above the neighboring landmark, the late nineteenth-century American Fine Arts Society (now Art Students League, one of the few remnants from 57th Street's art scene of the last century). This cantilever shifts the tower's center of gravity eastward slightly, so the tower can nab Central Park views around the Robert A.M. Stern building across the street.

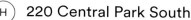

(H) 220 Central Park South

ROBERT A.M. STERN ARCHITECTS (RAMSA), 2018

Visible just beyond Central Park Tower is 220 Central Park South, whose 950-foot-tall (289 m) tower is positioned along 58th Street and the 18-story "Villa" is directly across the street from Central Park. Distinguished from the glassy supertalls along 57th Street by its limestone façade, the project recalls Robert A.M. Stern's earlier, nearby 15 Central Park West (15CPW) [6E]. Although One57 was the start of Billionaires' Row, it was 15CPW that paved the way for condo sales exceeding $3,000 per square foot. At 220 Central Park South, Stern continues the successful neo-traditional formula he started just across the corner of the park, this time giving the superrich views of each of its 843 acres (341 ha).

⋮ *Walk west to Eighth Avenue.*

(I) Hearst Tower

FOSTER + PARTNERS, 2006 – 300 WEST 57TH STREET

Even if it did not rise from a stone base dating to 1928, Norman Foster's triangulated design for Hearst Corporation would be one of the most striking tall buildings in New York City—in any city—completed this century. That it does sit literally inside the landmark that Joseph Urban designed for William Randolph Hearst can be chalked up to the fact that Urban planned it as the base for a tower—a tower never built due to the Great Depression. The Landmarks Preservation Commission (LPC) approved Foster's daring design in 2001 due in part to that 75-year-old plan; details on Urban's tower design were never discovered, leaving LPC open to a contemporary addition. By incorporating a diagrid exterior, which uses 20 percent less steel than a conventional post-and-beam frame, Foster turned Hearst Tower's 46 stories (six more than allowed by zoning after Hearst made improvement to the adjacent subway station) into a symbol of sustainability; the diagrid and other features earned the tower a LEED Platinum certification—the highest rating given in the US Green Building Council's program.

⋮ *Cross Eighth Avenue and walk to Hearst Tower's lobby.*

The LEED certification is proudly displayed at the entrance to the lobby, which is open to the public during business hours. Even though the atrium at the top of the escalators is not publicly accessible, from this lower level one can grasp how the tower is stabilized by diagonal bracing that echoes the exterior's diagrid, and how the old exterior walls have been propped up and incorporated into the soaring four-story space for Hearst's

employees. Richard Long's *Riverlines*, made by the artist with mud from the Hudson River and River Avon, and James Carpenter's *Ice Falls*, a cast-glass water feature that is fed by water collected on the roof, round out the lobby features.

> *Walk up to 57th Street, then left a few blocks to the corner of Eleventh Avenue.*

Kitty-corner is a full block with three buildings developed by the Durst Organization: at the corner is the 38-story Helena (FXFOWLE, 2005); to the right is Frank 57 West (Studio V, 2017) and beyond is BIG's VIA 57 West.

Cross Eleventh Avenue and 57th Street and walk to the mid-block drop-off.

(J) VIA 57 West

BJARKE INGELS GROUP (BIG), 2016 – 625 WEST 57TH STREET

The story goes that when Danish architect Bjarke Ingels introduced himself to NYC developer Douglas Durst in 2006, Ingels asked, "Why do all your buildings look like buildings?" It was a brash introduction, but one that managed to stick with Durst well enough that years later he hired Ingels's firm, BIG, to design a 700-unit rental apartment building on Manhattan's West Side. Overlooking one of the city's Department of Sanitation garages and the noisy West Side Highway, it was an ideal site for an introverted building; and that is what BIG delivered initially, in the form of a 15-story courtyard building. But with two doormen required and the building blocking views from the Helena, Ingels went back to the drawing board and devised a novel form that would fix those issues and result in a new hybrid: the "courtscraper," combining a European perimeter block and a Manhattan skyscraper.

The 34-story building starts as a one-story base along the south and west sides and ascends along its north and east sides to a 450-foot-tall (137 m) peak a full ten stories above the top floor of units. This leaning pyramid opens up views from the Helena and pushes the elevator core to the east end of the building, by the drop-off that bisects the block and unites Durst's three buildings. Apartments facing east and north (the latter toward Stanford White's landmark IRT Powerhouse from 1904) are angled relative to the double-loaded corridors inside, resulting in serrated glass-walled façades. The courtyard at the center of VIA 57 is visible from the drop-off, atop a flight of steps.

Walk west to Twelfth Avenue and cross 57th Street to the small triangle.

From this vantage point the swooping form of VIA 57 West is readily apparent, thanks in part to the 6,000 double-curved stainless-steel panels grouped into 1,200 mega-panels. Cut into these panels are terraces for the choice south-facing units, while units facing the courtyard have a similar serrated profile as the north and east elevations. Some treetops signal the western end of the courtyard—the same proportions as Central Park but 13,000 times smaller—whose surface slopes up counter to the

site's downward slope. Beneath the level of the courtyard is retail, parking, mechanical (above the 100-year floodplain), and plenty of amenities for the apartments, such as lounges, a pool, a basketball court, game room, and so forth.

To build an apartment tower on a former manufacturing site required a rezoning, which gave the local Community Board 4 some leverage to incorporate affordable housing. Durst complied—20 percent of the units are affordable for thirty-five years—and by doing so he received a 421-a tax break. Put another way, VIA 57 West was realized using legal and financial mechanisms much like the towers along Billionaires' Row. But the unprecedented architectural statement it makes points toward formal alternatives to reaching straight up to the sky.

End of tour. Want to backtrack to where Tour 6 starts? Walk one block east to just past Eleventh Avenue, board the M57 bus, and take it to Eighth Avenue.

6 Columbus Circle to Lincoln Center

1.5 MILES / 2.4 KM

> *This tour starts in front of Hearst Tower [51], a couple*
> *of blocks south of Columbus Circle, and ends a few blocks*
> *north of Lincoln Center.*

This tour traverses about a dozen blocks in the Lincoln Square neighborhood on Manhattan's Upper West Side. Anchored by a traffic node and a cultural institution, the area has a strong history of redevelopment that has shaped the blocks in and around Columbus Circle and Lincoln Center for the Performing Arts. In the middle of the last century, "Power Broker" Robert Moses set his sights on the area, parts of it then known as San Juan Hill, which he deemed suitable for two major developments: the New York Coliseum overlooking Columbus Circle and Lincoln Center, an arts campus occupying four full city blocks. Both used the federal government's Title I program, which launched in 1949 as a means of financing urban renewal projects in areas determined as slums; many of them, like San Juan Hill, were vibrant areas with minority residents unable to halt the march of "progress." Both of these major developments incorporated housing into adjacent parcels or blocks, but the main ingredients were large-scale venues for trade fairs and the performing arts.

The Coliseum, completed in the mid-1950s, came first. But, in Moses's words, "the scythe of progress must move north," and so it did with the groundbreaking of Lincoln Center in 1959 and its dedication ten years later. The Coliseum, as we'll see, didn't last into this century, while Lincoln Center's longevity required a transformation that turned the complex into a more inviting neighbor with active public spaces. Recent developments in Lincoln Square have balanced the commercial and retail uses lining Broadway with residential areas oriented more toward Central Park on the east and Amsterdam Avenue on the west. There is plenty to see in a relatively compact area.

> *Walk into the subway opening to the right of the Hearst Tower*
> *lobby, descend the stairs and follow them to the right.*

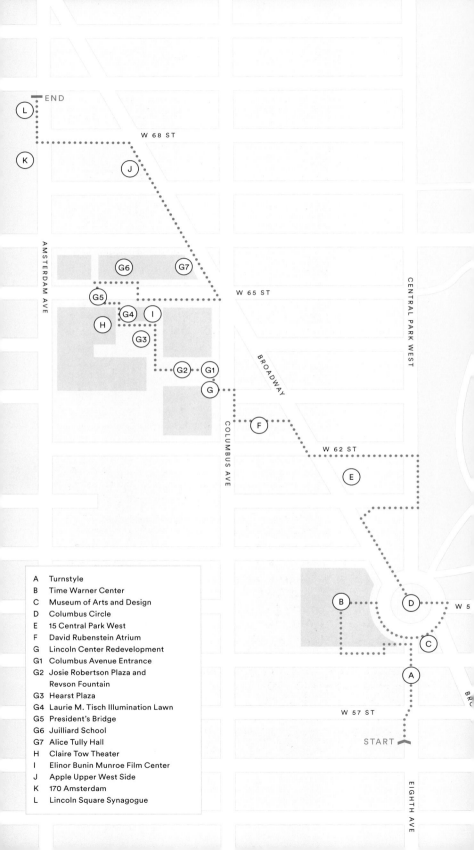

END

W 68 ST

AMSTERDAM AVE

CENTRAL PARK WEST

W 65 ST

BROADWAY

COLUMBUS AVE

W 62 ST

W 5

W 57 ST

START

EIGHTH AVE

L

K

J

G6 G7

G5

G4 I

H

G3

G2 G1

G

F

E

B D

C

A

A   Turnstyle
B   Time Warner Center
C   Museum of Arts and Design
D   Columbus Circle
E   15 Central Park West
F   David Rubenstein Atrium
G   Lincoln Center Redevelopment
G1 Columbus Avenue Entrance
G2 Josie Robertson Plaza and
      Revson Fountain
G3 Hearst Plaza
G4 Laurie M. Tisch Illumination Lawn
G5 President's Bridge
G6 Juilliard School
G7 Alice Tully Hall
H   Claire Tow Theater
I   Elinor Bunin Munroe Film Center
J   Apple Upper West Side
K   170 Amsterdam
L   Lincoln Square Synagogue

(A) Turnstyle

ARCHITECTURE OUTFIT, 2016 – 1000 EIGHTH AVENUE

This 200-foot-long concourse connects 57th Street to the five lines of the busy 59 Street–Columbus Circle subway station. The MTA decided in 2006 (the year of Hearst Tower, which paid for improvements to the station proper) to turn the long-empty mezzanine passage into retail, but it wasn't completed—under the moniker Turnstyle—until 2016. Developed by Susan Fine, who was responsible for the successful Grand Central Market at Grand Central Terminal, Turnstyle has around twenty small shops and eating establishments flanking the pedway, while small kiosks occupy the central spine alongside the riveted columns. Architecture Outfit's design adds some order via light, color, paint, and signage. Glass storefronts and transoms allow the individual establishments to grab the attention of passersby, but they also visually widen the space and highlight the scalloped ceiling. Along the central spine, laser-cut metal panels shield the lights and conceal the piping, while reflective panels tucked into the ceiling add some kaleidoscopic effects to the retail passage.

Walk to the northern end of Turnstyle and exit on the left via the escalator to street level.

(B) Time Warner Center

SKIDMORE, OWINGS & MERRILL (SOM); 2004 – 10 COLUMBUS CIRCLE

Overhead is the curving tip of the huge Time Warner Center (TWC), which occupies the two-block site of the former New York Coliseum. Created by the Triborough Bridge and Tunnel Authority under Robert Moses and designed by architects Leon and Lionel Levy, the Coliseum was a bland, blank-walled edifice— what Christopher Gray called "a low point for New York public buildings" in the *New York Times*—overlooking Columbus Circle. Completed in 1956, the Coliseum hosted more than one thousand shows before the opening of the Jacob K. Javits Convention Center near the northern tip of the High Line [TOUR 3] made it obsolete thirty years later. All that remains of the original project is the Coliseum Park Apartments along Columbus Avenue, which were included so Moses could secure Title I funds.

What was realized in its place two decades later (the Coliseum was not demolished until 2000) were two mixed-use towers above a retail base. Designed by SOM partner David Childs for the Related Companies, the 2.8-million-square-foot (260,000 sq m) project includes offices for Time Warner (with AOL at the time of completion), the Mandarin Oriental hotel, and condominiums in 53-story towers angled in plan like parallelograms to follow the grid and Broadway; with the Shops at Columbus Circle and Jazz at Lincoln Center in the curving base. Although Jazz at Lincoln Center clearly links Columbus Circle to Lincoln Center a few blocks up Broadway, it also harkens to the Majestic Theatre, which sat here from 1903 until the construction of the Coliseum and was a trailblazer in bringing the performing arts so far uptown.

Continue west along 58th Street to the entrance of the Shops at Columbus Circle. Go inside and follow the mall's curved walkway to the first escalator on the left. Head to the second floor and walk to the railing overlooking the atrium.

This vista reveals the curving arms of Time Warner Center's high-end mall, including its best architectural feature: a crystal clear, cable net glass wall facing Columbus Circle. Designed by glass artist/engineer James Carpenter, the wall was the largest of its kind when built. We see about only half of it: the rest extends above the ceiling, where it is hung from a large truss and layered in front of a second wall that encloses the performance spaces of Jazz at Lincoln Center and separates its sounds from those of the atrium.

Return to the escalators and descend to the ground floor. Walk toward the exit at the cable net glass wall, pause to look up at the two layers of glass walls, and then step outside.

(c) Museum of Arts and Design
ALLIED WORKS, 2008 – 2 COLUMBUS CIRCLE

This spot by the security bollards in front of TWC provides a good view of 2 Columbus Circle, better known as the Museum of Arts and Design (MAD). Built originally as Huntington Hartford's Gallery of Modern Art, Edward Durell Stone's 1964 design was described by *New York Times* architecture critic Ada Louise Huxtable as a "die-cut Venetian palazzo on lollipops," referring to the loggia formed by columns and circular accents around the base. Brad Cloepfil, head of Allied Works, removed Stone's marble façade in favor of iridescent tiles, filled the narrow corner windows, and cut new openings in apparently random lines up and across each elevation. The narrow windows continue inside as glass-filled gaps in the floors, like a continuous line that snakes its way around the compact building. Overlooking the Circle is a generous window that paints an "H" across the main façade; behind the window is Robert restaurant and its unimpeded views of Central Park.

Walk counterclockwise around Columbus Circle, crossing Eighth Avenue.

Walk inside MAD to get a closer look at the "lollipop" columns that remain (and the one removed to make way for the entrance).

*Exit and continue counterclockwise to the triangular
island in the middle of 59th Street and then cross west
into the middle of Columbus Circle.*

(D) Columbus Circle

OLIN, 2005

An apt label for people traversing the many lanes of traffic in
the last century to stand at the base of Gaetano Russo's 1894
sculpture of Christopher Columbus would have been daredevils;
such was the Circle's prioritization of cars over pedestrians.
Though not quite an oasis of calm in the city, the Circle's current
incarnation flips the priorities enough that it can be hard to recall
the asphalt-covered past. Landscape architect Laurie Olin was
working on much-needed alternatives to the traffic circle as far
back as 1980, but it wasn't until 2001 that he was hired to carry
out improvements that would be realized. Paid for by Related, the
redesign of Columbus Circle also included a tree- and bollard-
lined sidewalk in front of TWC. If Olin's design appears a bit safe,
this may be due to the myriad interests with a say in the Circle: the
MTA, since it sits above a major subway station; the Department
of Transportation; the Landmarks Preservation Commission; and
the Central Park Conservancy, among others. Although it has
some modern flourishes, such as the computerized fountains, the
landscaped Circle looks like a stable entity born of its place.

Access to the Circle happens at three points: eleven o'clock, seven o'clock, and three o'clock when seen on our map. Concentric rings of plantings, fountains, lighting, and benches reinforce the circular geometry while acting as layers of protection from the perimeter to the center. The landscaped berm provides enough soil for trees to grow above the subway station, but it also cuts down on the sound of traffic when seated at one of the generous, curved benches. In warm months, the dancing fountains, designed by WET, further mask the sound of cars and buses ringing the still-busy interchange.

Walk to the eleven o'clock access point, head to the east side of Broadway and walk north to the raised plaza between 60th Street and 61st Street.

This triangular space is part of the POPS (Privately Owned Public Space) that wraps the base of the Trump International Hotel and Tower and also includes a miniature Unisphere echoing the original from the 1964 World's Fair in Flushing, Queens. Built in 1969 as the Gulf & Western Building, the 44-story office tower was converted to a hotel and residences by Philip Johnson and Costas Kondylis, who clad the whole in bronze glass and stainless steel—signature Trump touches that attempted to overcome the original's aesthetic failings. This glitz was necessary, since tearing down the tower to build anew would have reduced the square footage allowable by zoning.

E 15 Central Park West
ROBERT A.M. STERN ARCHITECTS (RAMSA), 2008

Aligned with the plaza across 61st Street is another open space, a gap between two buildings covered in limestone. Not really empty, this space contains the motor court, copper-roofed entry, and below-grade common spaces for the 200 condominiums of 15 Central Park West, which are split into the 19-story "House" on Central Park West and the 35-story "Tower" on Broadway. Unlike the angled towers of TWC, RAMSA rotated the Tower along Broadway to align with the shorter House fronting Central Park. With this and other touches, such as the retail podium on Broadway that elevates the residences, the architects prioritized the views from apartments to Central Park over those of Broadway and Columbus Circle. Following from this, the condos, developed by William and Arthur Zeckendorf on the site of the Mayflower Hotel, set sales records and made the building notable for its residents more than its architecture; some of the big names have included Robert De Niro, Alex Rodriguez, Sting, and Denzel Washington. Russian billionaire Dmitry Rybolovlev purchased a ten-bedroom penthouse for $88 million in 2011, setting a record

for the most expensive apartment until the towers along
Billionaires' Row [TOUR 5] would take over.

> *Walk east along 61st Street and cross Central Park West into*
> *the small brick-paved plaza notched into Central Park.*

This small overlook provides a great view of Billionaires' Row
along 57th Street, including Stern's 220 Central Park South [5H],
and the top of his 30 Park Place across the east side of park.
In these projects, Stern—as much a historian as an architect (he
has written a handful of tomes on the city's architecture from the
mid-1800s to the millennium)—was inspired by early twentieth-
century apartment buildings in Manhattan, such as the San Remo
situated along Central Park West. At 15CPW, this translated into
façades of stone with small windows and bay windows rather than
all-glass curtain walls, a modest entry on Central Park West rather
than something flashy like Trump's glitz next door, and stepped
profiles (all the better for terraces) rather than boxy, modern
massings. Most distinctive is the asymmetrical top of the tower,
where a colonnade, buttresses, and other features present an
informal appearance when seen from the park—and make the rest
of us wonder about life at the top.

> *Walk up to 62nd Street, turn left and head west until you*
> *reach the northwest corner of Broadway; turn right and enter*
> *the David Rubenstein Atrium.*

(F) David Rubenstein Atrium

TOD WILLIAMS BILLIE TSIEN ARCHITECTS, 2009 – 61 WEST 62ND STREET

Before it was transformed into a climate-controlled space with
facilities for Lincoln Center, this POPS contained one of the
oddest amenities to be found in any urban public space, much
less a privately owned one: a climbing wall, facilitated by a nearby
sporting goods store. Timed to the 50th anniversary of Lincoln
Center, the space's transformation into the David Rubenstein
Atrium wrapped up in 2009 with booths for discount tickets and
guided tours of Lincoln Center, a sandwich shop, restrooms,
and plenty of tables and chairs.

Although Lincoln Center often closes the space for private
events, it is inviting and comfortable (the antithesis of its
predecessor), due in large part to the design by architects Tod
Williams and Billie Tsien. Most immediately striking are the
vertical green walls positioned near the entrances at Broadway
and Columbus Avenue (a third entrance to the T-shaped space
is located at 62nd Street). Between these patches of green are
yellow-and-gray felt murals by Claudy Jongstra on opposite walls.
A ceiling with circular skylights stretches the length of the space

and extends into canopies jutting over the sidewalk, beckoning visitors inside. Lastly, a fountain near the Lincoln Center visitor desk, with water dripping from a grid of metal rods, adds some soothing sounds to the space's visual softness.

Continue west through the atrium to Columbus Avenue, turn right to 63rd Street and cross Columbus.

(G) Lincoln Center Redevelopment

DILLER SCOFIDIO + RENFRO (DS+R), 2011

Lincoln Center for the Performing Arts, the main component of the 43-acre (17.4 ha) Lincoln Square Title 1 development, was enabled by the clearance of the tenements of San Juan Hill, the Puerto Rican neighborhood captured for the ages in the 1961 musical film *West Side Story*. Although the idea of a music and arts center dated back to 1938 and the wishes of Mayor Fiorello La Guardia, it didn't move forward until planning commissioner Robert Moses recognized two decades later that the arts had value in city building and that nonprofits had a tough time with Manhattan real estate. Under the leadership of John D. Rockefeller III (an odd choice, given his dislike of arts, music, and modern architecture) and following a master plan by Wallace Harrison, Lincoln Center was dedicated in 1969 with buildings for the New York City Ballet, the Metropolitan Opera, and the New York Philharmonic, among others. These three main components— designed by Harrison, Philip Johnson, and Max Abramovitz,

respectively—sit atop a huge plinth that contains parking, loading, and other services, and front the plaza that is reached by the wide steps from Columbus Avenue.

(G1) Columbus Avenue Entrance, 2010

With their LED, ticker-tape risers, these steps clearly aren't the ones that greeted visitors to Lincoln Center during its first four decades. As part of the numerous small- and medium-scale interventions that DS+R completed on the 16-acre (6.5 ha) campus between 2009 and 2012, the at-grade car drop-off was submerged and the 180-foot-wide (54.8 m) steps were brought closer to Columbus Avenue, turning an auto-centric approach into one that invites pedestrians to gracefully ascend the steps to the generous plaza and fountain beyond. The steps are flanked by accessible ramps covered by slender glass canopies that reach all the way to the curb, aligned to crosswalks across Columbus. The canopies are slotted into the loggias of the David H. Koch Theater (ballet) on the south and the David Geffen Hall (philharmonic) on the north, as the Met Opera beckons between the two in the distance.

⋮   *Walk up the steps to plaza level.*

(G2) Josie Robertson Plaza and Revson Fountain, 2010

Plans for the $1 billion transformation of Lincoln Center were announced in 1999 and three years later Diller + Scofidio was selected as the winner in an invited competition (Charles Renfro would join Elizabeth Diller and Ricardo Scofidio as name partners in 2004). The choice was surprising since the firm had built very little beyond set designs, installations, and interiors at the time (the first phase of their High Line design would break ground in 2006), and because they were up against some heavyweights: Santiago Calatrava, Norman Foster, Frank Gehry, and Richard Meier. But imagine a huge canopy over this plaza; that would be the reality if Gehry were selected. He and the other contenders saw the original Lincoln Center as a problem that required big solutions, while DS+R admitted to liking the "Acropolis for the cultural elite" and strove to "turn the campus inside out by extending the spectacle within" into the previously "mute" public spaces.

DS+R worked with FXFOWLE and Beyer Blinder Belle on various components realized in phases. Their sometimes minimal, almost invisible interventions are apparent in the trio of distinct but connected outdoor spaces completed in 2010: the entrance at Columbus Avenue described above, Josie Robertson Plaza, and Hearst Plaza. The second was designed by Philip Johnson in the original plan to echo Michelangelo's famed Campidoglio in

Rome, with light and dark stone patterns radiating from a central fountain. Water damage and outdated infrastructure necessitated new paving and a new fountain, but the replacements are true to the originals. In the case of Revson Fountain, numerous alternatives were explored, but the designers stuck with a circular shape. Lit from below, the ring suitable for sitting appears to float above the paving. Waterworks designed by WET add some theatricality to what remains the liveliest space at Lincoln Center, one that everybody should experience in the evening when arts patrons flood the space and the balconies overlooking it.

Walk west toward the Met Opera then right to the edge of Hearst Plaza.

(G3) Hearst Plaza, 2010

Like Damrosch Park to the south of the Met Opera, the great landscape architect Dan Kiley designed the former North Plaza. It then consisted of a grid of London plane trees (replaced later with pear trees), the 200-foot-wide (60.9 m) Paul Milstein Plaza over 65th Street, and a reflecting pool with Henry Moore's *Reclining Figure*. Due to extensive water damage leading to a plaza overhaul in 2010, only the last remains, in a subtly reworked form, while the pear trees were removed in favor of London planes once again, and the bridge was taken out to bring sunlight to the long-dark 65th Street. Hearst Plaza's design details express how DS+R addressed the 18-inch (45.7 cm) change in grade that was previously dealt with via awkward steps and slopes; now a gradual slope prevails. In turn, the reflecting pool and paving don't align, making the first look like a plane tilting at its own angle; and custom benches act as retaining walls for the Barclays Capital Grove (naming rights galore!), which is accessed by steps on the east but is flush on the west.

(H) Claire Tow Theater

H3 HARDY COLLABORATION ARCHITECTURE, 2012 –
150 WEST 65TH STREET

To the west, directly across the pool, is a layer cake of three functions: the Vivian Beaumont Theater (Eero Saarinen, 1965) at plaza level; the stacks of the New York Public Library for the Performing Arts in the cantilevered, travertine-clad upper story (interiors by Gordon Bunshaft/SOM, also 1965); and Hugh Hardy's addition of the Claire Tow Theater on the roof. Hardy's firm was responsible for an extensive interior renovation of the Beaumont Theater and then slated with adding a 112-seat theater in the only spot at Lincoln Center deemed acceptable for it. Accommodating an intimate theater for LCT3, which puts on plays by emerging playwrights, the new theater is perched on some of the original concrete columns, spanning them with 20-foot-deep (6.1 m) Vierendeel trusses that can be glimpsed through the glass walls wrapped in aluminum louvers. Entrance to the theater happens at new glass-enclosed elevators that cut through the floors of the Beaumont and NYPL.

> *Walk between the grove and pool to the Beaumont lobby*
> *and take the elevator to see the Claire Tow lobby, the green*
> *roof just outside the glass walls, and the view of the*
> *Tisch Illumination Lawn. Take the elevator back down*
> *to plaza level and walk north.*

(G4) Laurie M. Tisch Illumination Lawn, 2010

Before it took on its official name, DS+R called the building capped by the Tisch Illumination Lawn the "Hypar Pavilion." This name refers to the shape of the roof, a hyperbolic paraboloid: a curved surface made up of two straight-line parabolas. Rectangular in plan, the shape resembles a saddle and is an alien presence among Lincoln Center's predominantly orthogonal lines. Though often closed to recuperate after periods of use, the lawn is a welcome replacement to Milstein Plaza, which was underused at plaza level and shunned at street level. Below the accessible lawn is the Lincoln Ristorante. At plaza level, its dining room and display

kitchen are visible behind all-glass walls supported by glass fins, while the entrance and main kitchen are located at street level. Not visible is the kitchen's exhaust, which snakes itself around the building and exits through louvers by the parking garage entrance, visible near the entrance to the lawn.

After traversing the lawn, walk past the corner of the Beaumont Theater to cross over 65th Street.

(G5) President's Bridge, 2012

Although this slender bridge was the last piece to be completed in the Lincoln Center Redevelopment, 65th Street is really where the project began, with the demolition of Milstein Plaza in 2006. With that wide connection removed, people had to move subsequently between the renovated north and south sections of Lincoln Center at street level—now a welcoming scenario given the improved streetscape and new mid-block stoplight. The changes to 65th Street, discussed below, were dramatic enough that the need for a replacement bridge was debated; ultimately it was included for reasons of safety. DS+R's welded steel-plate bridge combines surface and structure in one; only glass guardrails depart from the gray steel palette. Set perpendicular to the street where it meets the Juilliard and Rose Building on the north, the bridge bends in plan to move people to and from the main plazas on the south. A third leg props up the bridge against the travertine wall next to the Beaumont Theater.

Cross the bridge, turn right and walk to the end of the outdoor walkway, then head inside through the doors on the left. Walk forward, turn right, and sit down on the steps.

(G6) Juilliard School, 2009

DS+R's work on the prestigious Juilliard School consisted of renovations to Pietro Belluschi's Brutalist original from 1969 and a dramatic expansion toward Broadway above Alice Tully Hall. For the former, the most overt change happens here at the entrance. Previously reached via the raised Milstein Plaza, the new entrance delivers students from the street to the second floor by what the architects describe as a "stair/hangout space in which risers morph into couches." Besides the grand stair and its undulating surfaces of wood is a new box office, while a walkway wraps beneath the stair as a small display space.

Exit at street level and cross 65th Street.

(I) Elinor Bunin Munroe Film Center
ROCKWELL GROUP, 2011

Tucked below the Lincoln Ristorante, in an old garage space, is a new venue for the Film Society of Lincoln Center, whose 268-seat Walter Reade Theater is located across 65th Street. The Elinor Bunin Munroe Film Center, designed by David Rockwell, consists of two theaters, an amphitheater, and a café. The recessed storefront, with its orange glass and angled canopy, appears to fold the flat façade of the DS+R pavilion. Walk inside the publicly accessible lobby, which is highlighted by views to the amphitheater through a 16-foot-wide (4.8 m) opening with a folding garage door that harkens to the space's previous use but is detailed with maple to match the space beyond.

Exit and head east alongside the "Infoscape," stopping at the base of the steps from Hearst Plaza.

This spot affords a couple views: of the east façade of the Lincoln Ristorante, whose roof roughly follows the angle of the stairs; and the extension of Juilliard School across the street. DS+R took the travertine façade of Belluschi's original and continued it to a point at Broadway, but they played around with the solid/void. The small windows on the top floor are consistent, but due to the insertion of a new floor below, the recesses and windows don't align.

Oddly, the windows wrap the edges of the progressively shallower travertine recesses, turning typically two-dimensional planes into three-dimensional surfaces.

⋮ *Continue east to Broadway and cross 65th Street to the corner.*

(G7) Alice Tully Hall, 2009

One of the first parts of the Lincoln Center Transformation was its most dramatic: the "completion" of the triangle between the old Juilliard School/Alice Tully Hall building and Broadway. Pietro Belluschi's original building was squared off perpendicular to the grid, leaving the leftover space as a plaza and unceremonious entrance to Alice Tully Hall beneath stairs that led to Milstein Plaza. With the latter's removal and the activation of 65th Street through reworked entries and new facilities, this plaza became a free canvas for a grand gesture by DS+R. Juilliard School was extended to the corner behind a taut glass façade facing Broadway. An angled ceiling accentuates the prow-like extension and highlights a studio for the School of American Ballet that projects through the 45-foot-tall (13.7 m) cable glass wall that wraps the corner. A sunken plaza with "Infopeel" steps at the corner leads to the café and lobby beyond the glass wall. The presence of Alice Tully Hall's Starr Theater beyond is expressed in dark wood walls that hint at its refashioned interior: African moabi veneer "blushes" from lights embedded within

the walls. Unable to isolate the sounds of passing trains within or underneath the hall, the MTA welded 1,000 feet (304 m) of rail on new concrete rails—as in other parts of Lincoln Center, some of the most beneficial changes are invisible to the public and arts-goers alike.

Walk up Broadway to 67th Street.

(J) Apple Upper West Side

BOHLIN CYWINSKI JACKSON, 2009 – 1981 BROADWAY

Of the seven Apple stores in Manhattan, this location can boast its own patent. The glass steps of many of the stores are patented, but in 2011 Steve Jobs filed a patent for "the ornamental for a building exterior." Although the glass cube of Apple's 24-hour NYC flagship on Fifth Avenue near Central Park is more recognizable, the 40-foot-tall (12.2 m) glass walls supported by glass fins are impressive; from inside they frame an expansive view of the surrounding high-rises. The glass roof, the stone walls bookending the large space, and the location of most of the wares in the basement accentuate the effect.

Walk up Broadway and turn left at 68th Street
to Amsterdam Avenue.

(K) 170 Amsterdam

HANDEL ARCHITECTS, 2015

With Manhattan's famous 1811 grid drawing streets above 14th Street from river to river, it's rare to find a building visually terminating an east-west street. One instance happens here, where 68th Street ends at Amsterdam Avenue and the 20-acre (8 ha) Lincoln Towers superblock, spanning from 66th to 70th Streets. While Lincoln Towers was built as part of the Lincoln Square Urban Renewal Area in the middle of the last century (*West Side Story* was filmed in the empty buildings that were torn down to make way for it), the apartment towers along the west edge of Amsterdam Avenue are more recent. Most striking is this 20-story building with 236 high-end residences designed by Handel Architects for Equity Residential.

Faced with a narrow lot, the architects moved the structural frame to the exterior to free up floor space in the units. The resulting concrete diagrid exoskeleton gives the building its can't-miss expression; without it, the slab of concrete floors and full-height window walls would be mundane. A couple of details further give the building some apparent dynamism: the intersections of the columns shifts one floor per bay, giving the impression that the diagrid is leaning; and the structure

extends past the roof to create an open framework and to partially shield the mechanical penthouse. Although its function is entirely different, it's hard to imagine 170 Amsterdam existing in this form without the precedent of Norman Foster's Hearst Tower at the start of this tour.

(L) Lincoln Square Synagogue
CETRARUDDY, 2014 – 180 AMSTERDAM AVENUE

Directly north of 170 Amsterdam is the new, larger home for Lincoln Square Synagogue, which was located one block north from 1970 until 2013. (The move was enabled by a land swap that will see a 55-story residential tower rise on the

site of the deconsecrated, demolished synagogue.) The design by CetraRuddy features five bands of undulating glass across the façade to symbolize the five books of the Torah. Bronze-colored fabric laminated to the glass is meant to evoke the parchment of Torah scrolls and the fabric of prayer shawls. Combined with the stone bookends, the building has an earthy, striated presence that changes in the evening when the glass glows like a lantern—something spiritual in a neighborhood of culture and commerce.

End of tour. For Tour 7, walk a few blocks up Amsterdam Avenue to take the 1 Train from 72nd Street to 116th Street.

7 Columbia University and Barnard College

1.5 MILES / 2.4 KM PLUS SUBWAY RIDES

⟩ *This tour starts at the gates to Columbia University, on the east side of Broadway at 116th Street, and ends in Washington Heights, at the Columbia University Medical Center. It involves three subway rides.*

Columbia University in the City of New York—the full name of New York State's oldest university—may be associated with its 32-acre (13 ha) campus in Morningside Heights, but Columbia has four other campuses: three farther north in Manhattan and one in the Hudson Valley. With few parcels available for new construction on its main campus in this century, this tour hits the three other campuses accessible by the 1 Train: Columbia University Medical Center in Washington Heights; Baker Athletics Complex in Inwood; and the Manhattanville Campus under construction a half mile (0.8 km) up Broadway. Founded by charter in 1754 as King's College, Columbia moved twice from its original site adjacent to Trinity Church before arriving in Morningside Heights. Each move was northward, paralleling Manhattan's growth. Growing pains pushed Columbia College, its name as of 1784, to buy the land of the Bloomingdale Insane Asylum of the New York Hospital at 116th Street and Broadway. In 1896, one year before it moved to its new, though partially completed campus, the school changed its name, finally, to Columbia University.

Of interest here is the campus master plan by McKim, Mead & White. Seth Low, Columbia's president at the time of the Morningside move, held a competition, with Charles McKim's firm besting Charles C. Haight, Richard Morris Hunt, and Frederick Law Olmsted Jr. with what could be described as the cheapest solution. Instead of stone, brick was the primary material, accompanied by limestone accents and copper roofs; Columbia's Morningside campus is the largest collection of McKim, Mead & White buildings anywhere, but their relatively austere exteriors (planned and designed largely by McKim) point to them never being landmarked. Another reason for the victory was the plan—buildings aligned to the streets and parallel buildings behind them creating smaller courtyards adjacent to

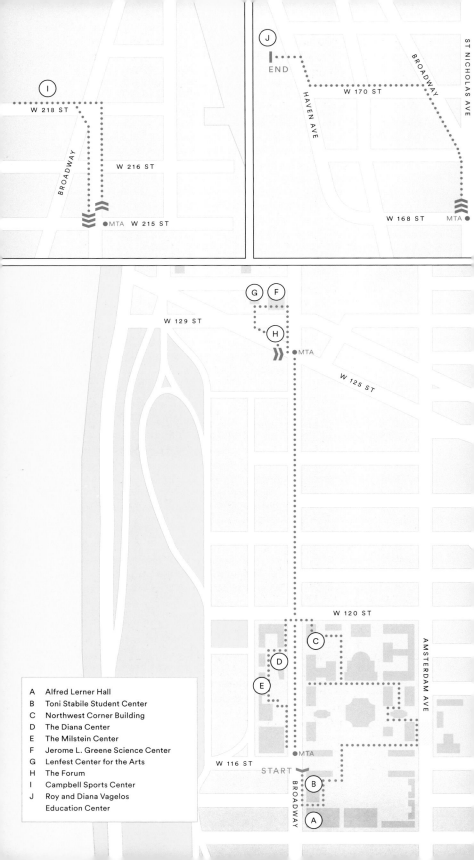

J   END

W 170 ST

BROADWAY

ST NICHOLAS AVE

HAVEN AVE

W 168 ST   MTA

I

W 218 ST

BROADWAY

W 216 ST

W 215 ST   MTA

G   F

W 129 ST

H

MTA

W 125 ST

W 120 ST

C

D

E

AMSTERDAM AVE

W 116 ST

MTA

START

BROADWAY

B

A

A   Alfred Lerner Hall
B   Toni Stabile Student Center
C   Northwest Corner Building
D   The Diana Center
E   The Milstein Center
F   Jerome L. Greene Science Center
G   Lenfest Center for the Arts
H   The Forum
I   Campbell Sports Center
J   Roy and Diana Vagelos
     Education Center

a larger central quadrangle—which could be built in phases as money and enrollment grew. Eventually the master plan would be just partially built out, with only one of the courtyards completed. Originally designed for the blocks north of 116th Street, just a decade later Columbia decided to extend the master plan two more blocks to the south.

Walk down Broadway to the sidewalk by the side gate at 115th Street.

(A) ## Alfred Lerner Hall

BERNARD TSCHUMI ARCHITECTS, 1999 – 2920 BROADWAY

Old and new face off across this narrow walkway: on the left is Furnald Hall, a dormitory designed by McKim and built in 1913; on the right is the student center designed by Bernard Tschumi and completed 86 years later. Tschumi's building is a good neighbor, matching the older building's height, materials, and major lines of composition; even Furnald's stone bullnose three floors up is carried through to Lerner Hall, but as curved pieces of glass block. This contextual approach was surprising coming from Tschumi, then the dean of Columbia's avant-garde Graduate School of Architecture, Planning and Preservation (GSAPP) and known best for the deconstructivist Parc de la Villette in Paris. He reserved the *différence* for the campus side.

Walk through the gate and up the walkway to the steps on the left.

Lerner Hall replaced Ferris Booth Hall, an unremarkable, unloved building from 1960 that served as a student center but was too small. Tschumi looked back in time beyond it, to the campus's master plan, and decided to use the largely unrealized courtyards as a means of organizing the building. (We are in one such courtyard—just imagine the hedge-framed lawn east of here as another McKim brick building.) In theory he created three buildings: the eight-story, contextual volume on Broadway; a parallel, four-story building in brick and stone on the campus side; and a glazed volume filling the gap in between. The auditorium fits into the last, while a campus bookstore, a cinema, a club, cafés, and other functions fit into the other two volumes. Visible behind the "courtyard's" glass wall are ramps that connect the half-level difference of the two brick buildings, matching the slope of the walkway we ascended from Broadway.

Although the glass wall's surface enables the courtyard metaphor to be grasped only at night, its construction and that of the ramps, also of glass, are impressive engineering feats. Two trusses span the 100 feet (30 m) between the base buildings on Broadway and the campus side to support the vertical loads for the glass wall and ramps. Engineered by Hugh Dutton, one truss is out of sight, at the roof, and holds up the ramps via tie-rods on their far edge. The second is a three-story inclined truss that holds up the front edge of the ramps (its incline matches that of the ramps). The glass wall is supported by spider fittings—the first such application in the United States—that reach out from the ramps on steel arms.

Walk up the steps and along Furnald Hall to the top of the steps fronting Pulitzer Hall.

(B) ## Toni Stabile Student Center
MARBLE FAIRBANKS, 2008

A glass wall is also an important aspect of this insertion between Furnald and Pulitzer, but in a much different manner. The project, designed by the firm of Scott Marble and Karen Fairbanks, comprises two parts: the renovation of a student lounge inside Pulitzer and a much smaller addition in the adjacent, formerly outdoor space. The glass wall fronts the latter, and in good weather it opens, extending the café seating outdoors. A lower glass panel (19 feet wide by 8 feet 6 inches tall [5.8 x 2 m]) weighing 5 tons (4.5 tonnes) lifts via a motor and gears hidden beneath the floor. Inside, the space is naturally illuminated from above through full skylights, but a ceiling of corrugated steel—perforated with a cloud-like pattern—cuts down on heat gain. The walls are a mix of old and new: the former as Pulitzer's exposed exterior wall and the latter, opposite, as bands of felt and an LED ticker. Lastly, take a peek through one of the windows into Pulitzer to see the lounge's west wall, whose steel surface is a digitally perforated rendition of the building across Broadway.

Walk around Pulitzer, cross the College Walk and ascend the grand steps to the brick-paved area below the Alma Mater *statue.*

This spot affords a sweeping view of Columbia's main quadrangle, which is bookended by Low Library (Charles McKim, 1897) on the north, and its replacement, Butler Library (James Gamble Rogers, 1934), to the south. Its architecture, modeled on the Pantheon in Rome, is impressive (and worth a peek, if open), but its elevated position hints at steam tunnels and other infrastructure that link the buildings north of 116th Street at basement level. The low-rise view panorama to the south would be much different if two 20-story towers designed by I. M. Pei, hired in 1968 to develop a campus master plan, had been built. They would have flanked a five-level subterranean gymnasium in front of Butler, but Pei's plan was unpopular and neither gym nor towers were built.

: *Walk east up the stairs and along the walkway to Revson*
: *Plaza.*

While Pei was not able to "modernize" McKim's campus, an earlier plan by Harrison & Abramovitz for a new East Campus extension across Amsterdam Avenue was successful. It is home to the Law School, the School of International and Public Affairs, and a large dormitory. Connecting the two is Revson Plaza, which has views up and down the avenue as well as of the "backs" of the McKim buildings lining its western edge.

: *Walk to the north end of Revson Plaza, then left back to the*
: *main campus, stopping in front of St. Paul's Chapel.*

The small brick and mansard building south of the chapel is the only survivor of the Bloomingdale Insane Asylum. Relevant here, the tiny Buell Hall houses the Temple Hoyne Buell Center for the Study of American Architecture and a gallery for GSAPP. The brick-and-stone St. Paul's Chapel fits well into campus, but the design is most notable for the Guastavino tile vaults inside. Rafael Guastavino, with his Guastavino Fireproof Construction Company, developed a system for building self-supporting arches and vaults from tile and mortar, realizing more than 250 projects in NYC alone. Although Guastavino often worked with McKim, Mead & White, the chapel was designed by I. N. Phelps Stokes, the nephew of the chapel's donor.

: *Walk north and east around St. Paul's Chapel to the*
: *courtyard just north of it.*

At last, we find ourselves in the one courtyard realized per the original master plan. It sits between three McKim buildings—one of them, Avery Hall to the west, houses the architecture studios, library, and other facilities of GSAPP. But this space is not as it was when the trio of buildings were completed ca. 1912. Architect Alexander Kouzmanoff, completing the only noticeable component of I. M. Pei's master plan, extended Avery Library— the world's largest architecture library—beneath the plaza, which necessitated elevating the paved surfaces in the middle of the space and adding skylights at its edges. When it was completed in 1977, Paul Goldberger compared it to a suburban mall.

: *Walk to the north edge of courtyard, turn left and walk west*
: *to the lookout at Broadway.*

This perch 20 feet (6 m) above sidewalk level looks across Broadway to Barnard College and its two twenty-first-century buildings we'll encounter soon. The subtle articulation of the stepped atria on the façade of Weiss/Manfredi's Diana Center [D] can be glimpsed on the right, while SOM's taller Milstein Center [E] is beyond.

Walk back east then take the first left north past the stairs and stop on the plaza.

(C) Northwest Corner Building

RAFAEL MONEO, 2010 — 550 WEST 120TH STREET

In the 1960s, Columbia could neither force its way into Morningside Park to build a new gymnasium nor carry out I. M. Pei's proposed sunken gym by Butler Library. So the university turned to a site first proposed in the 1940s: the northwest corner of its original campus. Left empty in

McKim's master plan, the north edge of campus filled in intermittently from the 1920s onward, but the northwest corner remained empty come the early 1970s. In the middle of that decade the university completed Dodge Physical Fitness Center, which seems to meld the two unbuilt gyms: a three-story building at the intersection of Broadway and 120th Street but buried beneath a plaza on the campus side, thanks to the significant grade change.

Accessed via the stairs we walked by, Dodge was built with foundations for a future tower for sciences. A first pass was taken in 1982, when Columbia hired James Stirling and Michael Wilford to design the Chandler North Project (it would have connected to Chandler Hall, a McKim, Mead & White building to the south). They designed a contextual building with a flared cornice on Broadway and an angled mass supported by two huge trusses on the campus side, but the project died when its budget came in excessively high. Columbia followed with a piecemeal extension of Havermeyer Hall (next to the Dodge stairs) in the mid-1980s, but it would take two more decades—113 years in all—to fill the northwest corner.

Faced with basketball courts in the middle of his building's footprint, Spanish architect Rafael Moneo designed the Northwest Corner Building as a bridge spanning a 126-foot-long (38 m) gap. The means of bridging is written across its elevations: the diagonal lines on the checkerboard of aluminum panels express the steel bracing behind it (the bracing is best seen later from Broadway). Housing labs for physics, chemistry, biology, and psychology, the building rises 14 floors, 10 of them at or above plaza level; bridges connect the new building to Chandler Hall on the south and Pupin Hall to the east. Labs face Broadway, while offices—two floors for every lab floor—face the campus behind a glass curtain wall. Most striking from this side of the building is the transparent library at plaza level; its column-free space, mimicking the gym below, is made possible by the full-floor truss between it and the offices above.

Walk into the Northwest Corner Building through the revolving doors and take the escalator down to the café.

Though small, this space says as much about the building as its gridded façade does. Framing views of Teachers College and Union Theological Seminary across the street, the café's glass walls are free of the large steel columns and bracing, such as that visible next to the escalator. Not only is the whole café hung from above, the northernmost structural bay is cantilevered. This transparent space, echoed by one atop the building, is enabled by the building's bridge-like structure. Furthermore, these spaces at the bottom and top of the building face north— toward Columbia's expansion into Manhattanville.

*Walk down the stairs, exit the building to 120th Street,
and then cross to the west side of Broadway.*

Before we step into Barnard College's campus, take a full look at the west-facing lab façade of Moneo's building, particularly the apparently random assemblage of diagonal lines. Designed with the structural engineers at Arup, early schemes had symmetrical bracing, but the collaboration led to the final result, which uses the least amount of steel. The building's odd appearance is the result of structural forces—and forces that put a gymnasium in this corner of campus thirty-five years before.

*Walk a few steps south, turn right into the campus of
Barnard College and stop at the terraced lawn.*

Packed tightly onto four narrow blocks between 116th and 120th Streets, Barnard College formed in 1889 after Columbia University president Frederick A. P. Barnard failed to convince trustees to admit women, and writer Annie Nathan Meyer campaigned for a women's college. Though independent, Barnard has been an affiliate of Columbia most of its existence; it first operated out of a townhouse near Columbia's previous Midtown campus, and then when Columbia embarked to Morningside Heights, so did Barnard. The women's college moved to a 1-acre (.4 ha) plot at Broadway and 120th Street formerly owned by the New York Hospital, thanks to an anonymous donor. (The college's first building, Milbank Hall, to the north of us, reveals the donor: Elizabeth Milbank Anderson.) Barnard has expanded since the campus's opening in 1897 to encompass six buildings on four acres (1.6 ha).

(D) The Diana Center
WEISS/MANFREDI, 2010 — 3009 BROADWAY

Earlier, from the Columbia campus, we saw the Diana Center's flat terracotta-colored glass façade on Broadway, and here we see its campus side—three-dimensional both in the angled plan aligning the main entrance on the south with Milbank's courtyard on the north, and in the circulation hung off its façade. Erected at the same time as Moneo's naming-rights-free Northwest Corner Building, the Diana Center is named for Diana Vagelos, who graduated from Barnard and was a donor with her husband for the building's construction (they also gave money for Columbia's Vagelos Center [J]). The six-story building (one below grade) replaces the much smaller McIntosh Student Center from 1969, and in turn it adds educational spaces for art, architecture, and performance to those original functions. Designed by the firm of Marion Weiss and Michael Manfredi, the building's main spaces are organized about what they call a "stepped atria" that

is positioned along Broadway and ascends diagonally from the ground level on the south to the green roof on the north.

Ascend the path next to the terraced lawn, take a left and enter the Diana Center. Head up the second stair on the left and then turn right to the stepped atria.

The two side-by-side stairs next to the entry doors signal what is happening with the distinctive network of circulation. Outboard is a fire stair and inboard is an open, communicating stair; the former is necessary per building code, which requires exit stairs in fire-rated enclosures. Instead of treating the fire stairs in a typical, hidden manner, Weiss/Manfredi expressed them on the exterior and enlarged them so their landings could be used as spillover space from, for instance, adjacent architecture studios. Across the hall is the "stepped atria." What can be glimpsed either through the glass or inside is how each "step" is a distinct room separated from the ones above and/or below by full-height glass walls—as much for sound concerns as for fire separation. The four double-height spaces contain a café, a dining room, a reading room, and a gallery. The glass panes that separate the atria from the hallway are treated with a pinstripe frit similar to the terracotta lines on the exterior.

Walk back downstairs, exit the building and head to its south end.

Just as Barnard's affiliation with Columbia brought it to Morningside Heights, Barnard was built with a brick-and-stone architecture similar to McKim's buildings. The Diana Center fits into this context, but with glass instead of brick. Seen here up close, Weiss/Manfredi managed to detail the solid terracotta-colored panels so that the flat surfaces appear milky, and with depth. This effect is pulled off by treating them as shadow boxes: the glass has a matte, acid-etched surface on the outside and a terracotta-colored frit on the inside surface, and four inches (10 cm) behind it is a bright-red metal panel; the reflection of the latter on the glass produces the distinctive haze. Also visible here is the cantilever, the exclamation point of the circulation network on the building's west façade.

(E) The Milstein Center

SKIDMORE, OWINGS & MERRILL (SOM), 2018 – 3009 BROADWAY

At five stories on the south and eleven stories on the north, SOM's Milstein Center mediates between its neighbors, the 1917 Barnard Hall and 1969 Altschul Hall, respectively. The new building replaces and nearly doubles the size of Lehman Hall, a small modern building from the late 1950s that housed the Wollman Library. Now suited to the twenty-first century, the new Wollman Library is accompanied by a computer science center, classrooms, conference facilities, offices, and a café. Numerous terraces result from the stepping of the lower floors, which are covered in clear glass. The tower, on the other hand, is primarily solid, with horizontal windows set into shingled zinc panels that were patinated to evoke the weathered surfaces of older Barnard buildings. The ninth-floor cantilever, which houses the Salon and has panoramic views over campus, visually connects the building to the Diana Center across the lawn.

Walk south and exit Barnard's campus to the 116 St subway, taking the 1 Train north to 125th Street. Exit to the southwest corner of 125th Street and Broadway.

The realization of Columbia's 32-acre (13 ha) Morningside campus unfolded over decades, and the same applies to its 17-acre (6.8 ha) Manhattanville Campus, whose first buildings opened in 2017 and whose last will arrive by 2030, if all goes to plan. But unlike the single-owner situation of the Bloomingdale Insane Asylum, the four large blocks northwest of this intersection encompassed numerous owners of storage warehouses, garages, and other primarily industrial buildings. Columbia started buying up buildings on the footprint of its future campus even before University president Lee Bollinger announced the project in 2003. Although eminent domain had to be used to obtain the balance,

Columbia managed to buy most of the land—61 of 67 buildings on the blocks bounded by Broadway, Twelfth Avenue, 125th Street, and 133rd Street—successfully, despite community opposition and lawsuits dragging out the process. The impetus to build nearly 7 million square feet (650,000 sq m) of classrooms, labs, dorms, and other educational spaces was mathematical: Columbia had the lowest per student square footage in the Ivy League—half as much as Harvard, the next lowest. They also lacked facilities

for neuroscience, a conference center, and a decent art gallery, among other things.

Renzo Piano Building Workshop (RPBW) and SOM were hired in 2002 to develop the Manhattanville Campus master plan. Though twice as large, McKim's Morningside campus was a touchstone for the team. They went against it in a few ways: retaining the east-west streets; creating ground-level spaces that were porous, both visually and physically; and developing a modern, yet varied formal aesthetic arising from the involvement of various architects and the preservation of select old buildings. One consistency with the McKim campus was infrastructure. RPBW and SOM devised a huge, seven-story underground (built as a "bathtub" like the original World Trade Center) for parking, loading, mechanical, and myriad other services or functions not fitting into the new buildings. In essence, the buildings plug into and share the services of this expansive base, which in turn removes loading and other unsightly but necessary features from the ground floors, enabling them to be wholly transparent.

RPBW designed the first three buildings, described below, as well as a planned Global Center that will fill out the triangle below 130th Street. To the north, Diller Scofidio + Renfro has designed a pair of buildings for the Business School that will face each other across a large green space by James Corner Field Operations when completed in 2021. Two former, early twentieth-century automobile buildings sit on blocks to the north, but it's too early to know what new buildings will accompany those.

⁞ *Cross 125th Street and continue up Broadway to 129th Street.*

(F) ## Jerome L. Greene Science Center
RENZO PIANO BUILDING WORKSHOP (RPBW), 2017 – 3227 BROADWAY

Columbia's Manhattanville campus was officially dedicated on October 24, 2016, about six months before the Greene Science Center became the first building to open on campus. But long before it officially opened, its nine floors and twin stacks made a mark on the West Harlem surroundings. If the exhausts appear oversize for the science labs inside, it's because they rise from the Central Energy Plant in the basement.

Housing the Mortimer B. Zuckerman Mind Brain Behavior Institute, the square building organizes research labs in four quadrants divided by inset, intersecting axes: north-south is dedicated to circulation and east-west is given over to meeting rooms and other breakout spaces behind glass partitions. Double-layer glass façades ensure the rumble of the elevated trains aren't sensed by researchers and that natural light permeates into the deepest parts of the plan—not too much, though, as shades between the layers of glass are raised and lowered automatically

via sensors on the roof. At the top floor are a lecture hall
and an adjacent roof terrace with panoramic views, where
the top of Moneo's Northwest Corner Building [C] is visible.
Beneath the seven lab floors is a mechanical level cloaked
in Columbia-blue metal panels and the glazed first floor, home
to retail, an education center, a wellness center that area
residents can patronize free of charge, and a publicly accessible
lobby with an interactive wall installation.

Walk into the Science Center's lobby, try out the installation, and then walk through to the small plaza.

(G) Lenfest Center for the Arts

RPBW, 2017 – 615 WEST 129TH STREET

Opening soon after the Greene Science Center, the Lenfest Center for the Arts may seem like an odd fit with a building devoted to neuroscience, but it makes sense on at least two counts: Lenfest's spaces for exhibitions, films, performances, and other arts-related events are across the street from Prentis Hall, which houses some School of the Arts and Music Department studios; and the learning taking place in Manhattanville's first two buildings parallels the research of Columbia's own Eric Kandel, a neuroscientist who studies the neurological links between art and science. Uniting them here is the small plaza—*piazza* in Piano's Italian parlance—designed by landscape architect James Corner and the southern end of a north-south pedestrian spine that will eventually span the campus's four large blocks. Lenfest's four main components are stacked above the transparent lobby as double-height volumes behind light-gray metal walls and south-facing windows. From bottom to top are the windowless film screening room, the flexible performing space, the Miriam and Ira D. Wallach Art Gallery, and a flexible event space—the Lantern—beneath a roof of skylights. That each space is sized depending on its needs is evident in the cantilevers on the sides and the exposed steel columns below them.

Walk into the lobby and take the elevator to the publicly accessible Wallach Gallery, open Wednesdays to Sundays.

The Wallach Art Gallery moved from the recesses of Schermerhorn Hall (near Avery Hall) to this spacious home that displays student work and hosts exhibitions focused on contemporary artists at Columbia and the surrounding communities. The large gallery space has exposed ducts that snake through castellated steel beams, as well as the steel columns aligned with those we glimpsed outside. A large window looks to the north, though motorized shades block out natural light when needed.

Exit the building and cross 129th Street.

(H) The Forum

RPBW, 2018 – 605 WEST 125TH STREET

First science, then art; third on the Manhattanville campus is communication, in a three-story building with an auditorium, meeting rooms, offices, and gathering spaces, all catered to conferences and other events where scholars meet and present their work. Sitting on its own triangular island formed by the angle of 125th Street, RPBW designed the Forum as a gateway to the new campus, with an information center, cafés, and retail spaces on the transparent ground floor. Glass covers the upper two floors on the tapered, western end of the building, while precast concrete clads the taller volume on the east, where the auditorium is situated. In between are a south-facing terrace, exposed stairs, and a steel mast, all expressing the notion that the building is like a ship raised above the clear base.

> *Take the 1 Train north to 215th Street, walk up Tenth Avenue and then left on 218th Street.*

ⓘ Campbell Sports Center
STEVEN HOLL ARCHITECTS, 2013 – 533 WEST 218TH STREET

In 1922, the Baker Athletics Complex opened in Inwood, at the northern tip of Manhattan, and has since served as the primary facilities for the Columbia University Lions' outdoor sports teams (baseball, football, tennis, track, etc.). Although five miles (8 km) north of the Morningside campus, the complex is easily reachable via subway, and it takes advantage of its remote location with direct access to Spuyten Duyvil Creek for the rowing team. The Campbell Sports Center, at the southeast corner of Baker, is a gateway to the complex and the first sports building for Columbia since the Dodge Physical Fitness Center in 1974. The five-story building houses strength and conditioning spaces, coaches' offices, a study center, a hospitality suite, and a theater-style meeting room.

Holl, who develops concepts for each of his projects, looked to field play diagrams for such sports as football and designed

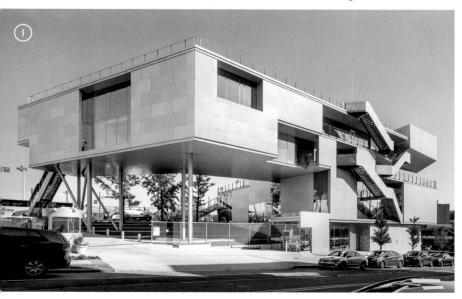

the building—the New York architect's first in Manhattan—as "points on the ground, lines in space." The lines are expressed in the terraces and stairs on the elevations facing both the streets and the fields. The points are evident, in plan at least, as the columns and diagonal supports that prop up the bridge-like wing with offices; a stair at the tip delivers the coaches to fields directly. The soffit of this bent wing, as well as the terraces and underside of the angled meeting room at the corner, is finished in Columbia blue, a subtle sign of the institution occupying this tip of the island.

Walk back to the 1 Train at 215th Street and take it south to 168th Street. Exit the station and walk up Broadway to 170th Street, then left to Haven Avenue.

(J) Roy and Diana Vagelos Education Center
DILLER SCOFIDIO + RENFRO (DS+R), 2016 – 104 HAVEN AVENUE

In June 2012, the *New York Times* reported on the unveiling of DS+R's design of a 14-story tower for the Columbia University Medical Center (CUMC), incorrectly attributing a rendering of the building's south façade as a "cutaway rendering," one where the skin is pulled off to reveal its internal spaces. The error is understandable, given the nature of renderings to depict glass in a highly transparent manner, but also due to the design: an atypical stacking of horizontal slabs, angled stairs, and floating terraces. Four years later, the built version came out astonishingly true to the rendering, revealing the so-called "study cascade" at the south end of the building behind clear, low-iron glass supported by glass fins.

The Vagelos Education Center is a standout building when seen from the south, but it is hardly unprecedented. The firm founded by Elizabeth Diller and Ricardo Scofidio has been trying to realize something like this since they won the competition for the Eyebeam Museum of Art and Technology in 2001. In that unbuilt project, a continuous ribbon of floors and walls rose from sidewalk to roof, with glass walls in between revealing the museum's various contents. Vagelos isn't quite a continuous ribbon, but the undulating surfaces of GFRC (glass fiber reinforced concrete) outside and Douglas Fir inside certainly recall Eyebeam; and the stairs stitching together the various parts of the Study Cascade effectively make it a continuous network of vertically linked spaces for collaboration and informal learning. North of the Study Cascade are the core and the classrooms, meeting rooms, labs, and other formal spaces of learning for the four CUMC schools that the building serves; these spaces sit behind glass façades with a frit pattern that appears milky and cuts down on direct sunlight.

(J)

*Cross Haven Avenue and walk toward the building,
then left and under the exterior stair to the small plaza
on top of the parking garage ramp.*

A walk past the Study Cascade gives a closer look at the GFRC panels that make up the façade, as well as the exposed concrete structure behind the glass. Designed with engineer Leslie E. Robertson, the slabs of the cascade cantilever from a pair of columns that follow the splayed section and lean inward at the base, by the lobby and auditorium. The latter space connects to a terrace overlooking the Hudson River and George Washington Bridge. This terrace, and the smaller ones that climb the Study Cascade, express how views *from the building* are as important as views *of it*.

*End of tour. Backtrack to the 168th Street subway station
for service on the 1, A or C Trains.*

8 Brooklyn Bridge Park

2 MILES / 3.2 KM

〉 *This tour starts in Dumbo at the Pearl Street Triangle and ends at the southern tip of Brooklyn Bridge Park.*

Brooklyn Bridge Park's combination of architectural design, varieties of landscapes and uses, and views of its namesake landmark and parts of Lower Manhattan make it one of the most satisfying landscapes built in the city in this century. Following the East River in a 1.3-mile (2.1 km) swoop from Atlantic Avenue near Brooklyn Heights to Jay Street in Dumbo, Brooklyn Bridge Park (BBP) is an 85-acre (34 ha) park made up of a series of smaller parks and piers for recreation and repose. Like the High Line [3B], BBP is self-supporting, but unlike the High Line's strong fund-raising, the nonprofit Brooklyn Bridge Park Corporation relies on a handful of development parcels to pay its roughly $16 million annual budget. This tour highlights the park design of Michael Van Valkenburgh Associates (MVVA), as well as the design of adjacent buildings, both development parcels and not.

Our starting point is in Dumbo, a factory and warehouse district that was transformed into a post-SoHo acronym neighborhood (Down Under the Manhattan Bridge Overpass) in the late 1990s. From the Civil War to mid-twentieth century, Arbuckle Coffee, E. W. Bliss Company, and other companies called the area home. Industries started moving out as early as the 1920s, and fifty years later artists started to move in, paving the way for development. Its current state can be attributed to one person: David Walentas, head of Two Trees Management. He bought up a dozen buildings in the early 1970s and converted them for commercial and residential uses. The appeal of the area—with its intact industrial buildings, Belgian-block streets, and the dramatic presence of the Manhattan Bridge (its anchorages designed by Carrère & Hastings)—is undeniable; no wonder more than a dozen blocks were made into New York City's 90th historical district by the Landmarks Preservation Commission (LPC) in 2007.

The spot we're standing in, Pearl Street Triangle, was a parking lot until 2007, when it was taken over by paint, planters, and

MANHATTAN BRIDGE

JOHN ST

PLYMOUTH

BROOKLYN BRIDGE

D1   D

E   C

D2

B

A

WATER ST

START

G

WASHINGTON ST

JAY ST

H

F

OLD FULTON ST

FURMAN ST

I

D4

D3

J

D5

K

REMSEN ST

HICKS ST

D6

ATLANTIC AVE

FERRY

END

A   Dumbo Townhouses
B   205 Water Street
C   10 Jay Street
D   Brooklyn Bridge Park
D1   John Street Park
D2   Main Street Park
D3   Squibb Bridge
D4   Pier 1
D5   Pier 3 Greenway & Berm
D6   Pier 6
E   One John Street
F   Empire Stores
G   Jane's Carousel
H   St. Ann's Warehouse
I   1 Hotel Brooklyn Bridge
J   Pierhouse
K   BBP Boathouse

tables and chairs. Though modest, it is notable as the Bloomberg administration's first car-to-pedestrian transformation under Department of Transportation commissioner Janette Sadik-Khan—two years before Times Square was pedestrianized.

(A) Dumbo Townhouses
ALLOY, 2015 – 55 PEARL STREET

A Dumbo oddity, these five five-story townhouses that replaced an old warehouse occupy a corner lot that could have been developed as a much larger building. In its first project, Alloy— the architecture and development firm started by Katherine McConvey and Jared Della Valle—opted to build low to reduce excavation costs and take out the common areas (corridors, elevators, mechanical shafts) necessary in tall buildings. With a palette of stainless steel and Ipe wood on the first floor and fiber cement panels above, the resulting building is a handsome addition to the neighborhood. Much of the character is derived from the fiber cement panels, which define narrow windows that get even narrower on the upper floors and give the residents of Dumbo's first—and only—townhouses some privacy from passersby.

Walk east on Water Street to Jay Street, then left to Plymouth Street.

(B) 205 Water Street

S9 ARCHITECTURE, 2012

Although the address of this 67-unit condo building for
Toll Brothers is on Water Street, it is best seen from the rear.
Look above the building's exposed-concrete frame to see
the two-story penthouse framed in Cor-Ten steel. The design
by S9 Architecture (drawn up when its two founding partners
were employed at GreenbergFarrow) has an exposed-concrete
frame and large windows to fit among the neighboring lofts,
while the rooftop piece was inspired by the nearby Manhattan
Bridge. In 2015 the penthouse was purchased by architect
Bjarke Ingels, who stated at the time it will afford him
a view of 2 World Trade Center [TOUR 1]—whenever its
construction happens.

*Continue up Plymouth Street to the northern tip
of Brooklyn Bridge Park.*

(C) 10 Jay Street

ODA NEW YORK, 2018

The only building of the 91 in the Dumbo Historic District that
sits north of John Street, this late nineteenth-century sugar
refinery was turned into a warehouse in 1945, and from the 1990s
until 2014 was occupied by tech companies. It was converted
by Eran Chen's ODA for Triangle Assets into a Class A office
building with a contemporary façade overlooking the East River.
The attention-getting façade was approved by LPC because
the northern half of the original building was demolished shortly
after its conversion into a warehouse, and the north façade was
filled in during the ensuing decades, ripe for reinvention. Inspired
by the building's first use, ODA designed this face like a crystal,
further conceptualizing the building as a geode—its landmarked
masonry encasing the new wall of faceted glass.

(D) Brooklyn Bridge Park

MICHAEL VAN VALKENBURGH ASSOCIATES (MVVA), 2010–2018

Even though the story of Brooklyn Bridge Park extends back to
the early eighteenth century, the decision to replace the formerly
industrial waterfront with a public park got its official start in 1997,
when the Downtown Brooklyn Waterfront Local Development
Corporation was established to develop a park plan. Limited
initially to the stretch of piers near Brooklyn Heights that the Port
Authority of New York and New Jersey closed to commercial
shipping in 1984, the plan was extended north to Dumbo in 1999
around the time developer David Walentas was trying to develop

his own (unsuccessful) commercial waterfront plan. The Brooklyn
Bridge Park Corporation was formed in 2002, when Governor
Pataki and Mayor Bloomberg signed a memo of understanding
for funding the park's construction. The corporation was slated
with funding the park's maintenance, and the chosen route
was to develop residential and commercial sites adjacent to the
park's ends and midsection.

(E) One John Street

ALLOY, 2016

Next to 10 Jay Street's "geode" is its apparent antithesis: a simple
cube of brick and glass. The product of a 2013 RFP (request
for proposals) won by Alloy with Monadnock Construction,
One John Street sits on the northernmost development parcel
in Brooklyn Bridge Park. The 12-story building contains 42
apartments and, on its ground floor, Spark, an annex of the
Brooklyn Children's Museum. Columns ring the ground floor and
express the structure that is otherwise hidden behind the grid
of windows above. A few subtle details worth noting: the windows
get smaller as the building gets taller, in response to noise from
the Manhattan Bridge and increased sunlight exposure at the
upper floors; these same windows look fixed, but in fact they
open slightly as awnings; and the bricks that sit between the
protruding windows are handmade in Denmark, developed out
of a museum in Cologne, Germany, designed by Peter Zumthor.
While all of the residents are graced with unencumbered

water views thanks to BBP, park-goers are treated to fractured reflections of the Manhattan Bridge and surroundings off the building's grid of windows.

(D1) John Street Park

MVVA, 2015

Landscape architect Michael Van Valkenburgh's firm was hired in 2003 to design BBP, but its first sections wouldn't open until 2010, with its last pieces expected in place by 2018. This northernmost park was completed in 2015, just before the completion of One John Street. Only two blocks wide (from Jay Street to Adams Street), the park is small but full of character: it has a bridge over the water at Jay Street, a 13,000-square-foot (10,869 sq m) lawn, and a tidal salt marsh that fills during high tide and storm surges. The last is highlighted by the insertion of some old industrial footings that were found during construction. At the western end, toward the Manhattan Bridge, is an overlook with benches and information on the Billion Oyster Project. The community science project aims to add one billion live oysters to 100 acres (40 ha) of reefs in New York Harbor by 2030—just a small fraction of the 220,000 acres (89,000 ha) covered by oysters before European settlement.

Follow the shoreline past the climbing boulders to the Environmental Education Center at the end of Washington Street, under the bridge.

This small building houses an educational center (with a model of BBP), community spaces, and restrooms. The city-owned building was donated to BBP as part of negotiations to realize St. Ann's Warehouse [H].

Walk alongside the playground to the curved steps and small beach.

(D2) Main Street Park

MVVA, 2015

Although BBP stretches for nearly 1.5 miles (2.4 km) along two neighborhoods—Brooklyn Heights and Dumbo—it has only three primary entrances: active nodes where playgrounds and the like are clustered. One of these is Main Street Park, with a nautically themed playground, a dog run, and the playground for adults that is the Boulders. There are places for repose as well: a lawn, a promenade along the rocky shoreline, and the seating area next to Pebble Beach that invites people to gaze at the Brooklyn Bridge with Lower Manhattan beyond it. This spot affords a good view of the next two buildings.

Continue down the shoreline to the courtyard entrance
of the Empire Stores.

(F) Empire Stores

STUDIO V ARCHITECTURE & S9 ARCHITECTURE, 2017 –
53–83 WATER STREET

This string of warehouses dating back to 1869 is considered the first commercial production facility for roasted coffee. Filling a whole block, the Empire Stores sit within the Fulton Ferry Historic District, which LPC designated in 1977, forty years before the Dumbo Historic District. The restoration that accompanied Midtown Equities's transformation of the 400,000-square-foot (37,161 sq m) block into offices, retail, restaurants, and cultural and public spaces has made the long-vacant structures useful again and given BBP another revenue stream for its hefty maintenance costs. Much of the square footage behind the arched openings adorned with shutters is occupied by West Elm, which also has a store on the ground floor.

Take the glassed-in elevator, located at the edge of
the courtyard, to the roof.

Empire Stores is exceptional for its porosity, both architecturally and in terms of public access. The carving of a courtyard into the center of the block invites the public into the realm of the

primarily commercial project. In addition to providing a thru-block connection to Water Street, this outdoor space leads to a Brooklyn Historical Society branch on the second floor and a public roof terrace. Though relatively small compared to the footprint of the block-long buildings, the public rooftop designed by Future Green provides people a place to rest and enjoy higher views of the skyline, the river, the park, and Jane's Carousel below.

Head downstairs, walk back to BBP and head to the carousel seen from the roof.

(G) ## Jane's Carousel
ATELIERS JEAN NOUVEL, 2011

In 1984, developer David Walentas's wife, Jane, bought a 1922 carousel at an auction after an amusement park in Youngstown, Ohio, closed. French architect Jean Nouvel designed the simple boxy enclosure that sits next to Empire Fulton Ferry Lawn (formerly a state park but added to BBP in 2010) on an elevated plinth that houses electrical and mechanical equipment. Four round columns support a roof that is punctuated by a glass skylight the same size as the carousel. Full-height sliding walls open the space to the elements and enable breezes on warm days. Walls—both fixed and sliding—look like glass from a distance, but are actually acrylic, a lightweight alternative that is evident upon touch.

Even with the carousel propped up on a plinth, Hurricane Sandy caused $300,000 worth of damage in 2012, cresting above the plinth and inundating the services in the cellar. Following repairs, the Walentases (who have endowed the carousel's maintenance costs) bought "aqua fences" that would be installed during the next storm surge—practically a guarantee given its location.

Walk south a few steps.

St. Ann's Warehouse

MARVEL ARCHITECTS, 2015 – 45 WATER STREET

Though small, this rectangular building and adjoining triangular courtyard are one of the most controversial aspects of Brooklyn Bridge Park. Built as a tobacco storage facility around the same time as the Empire Stores, the five-story building was trimmed when the Brooklyn Bridge was built in the 1880s and cut down to two stories in the 1940s. Three decades later the building was gutted in a fire and sat as an empty shell until this century, when tents were erected inside for interim performances. Controversy came in 2010 when nonprofit St. Ann's Warehouse, established in Brooklyn Heights in 1980, won an RFP with developer David Walentas to convert the old structure into a permanent performing arts space. A couple of lawsuits from community groups followed and a judge ruled that the building could not be converted, since it sat on federally protected land (this ruling applied to Empire Stores too). Ensuing negotiations between the city, state, and National Parks Service effectively overturned the decision and set the buildings on course for conversion. With arched openings in brick walls punctuated by tie-rods, the building is akin to Empire Stores. A glass-brick clerestory that pops above the old warehouse's remaining two stories gives St. Ann's a bit of pizzazz, especially when it glows after sundown. The design by the firm of Jonathan Marvel squeezes a 700-seat theater, offices, and support spaces inside, with plywood-lined walls standing out from the brick shell.

The building's restrooms and other service spaces are aligned toward the courtyard designed by Michael Van Valkenburgh and christened the Max Family Garden. Serving as spillover space during performances, the triangular garden is an intimate respite from the crowds in BBP. Paths meander among trees and seats made from locally salvaged blocks of bluestone.

*Exit the garden at the tapered end by Water Street,
turn right and walk down to where Old Fulton Street
meets Furman Street.*

The pier at the end of Old Fulton Street served as the landing for Robert Fulton's ferry, which operated from 1814 to 1924. At its peak in the 1850s, more than half of Brooklyn's 300,000 residents took the 12-minute ride daily to and from Manhattan, near today's Pier 17 [1E]. Fulton's business helped make Brooklyn Heights—high above the industrial piers extending south from the landing—a desirable place for the wealthy to live. No built structures remain from Fulton's 110-year-long operation, but the Brooklyn City Railroad Company building overlooking this intersection harkens to that pre-Brooklyn Bridge era when the company operated horsecar lines that moved people to and from the ferry.

*Walk south along Furman to the canopy and wood-lined
portal on the right.*

1 Hotel Brooklyn Bridge

MARVEL ARCHITECTS, 2017 – 60 FURMAN STREET

The development site at BBP's midsection is long and slender, stretching about four blocks on the footprint of some old warehouses. Developed jointly by Toll Brothers and Starwood Capital Group, the project is separated into two parts: Pierhouse's 106 condominiums [J] on the south and the 194-room 1 Hotel on the north. Given the project's length along Furman Street, the buildings are broken into two smaller volumes, with Squibb Bridge [D3] in between them, and are pierced by portals that connect Furman Street to BBP. Architect Jonathan Marvel's firm expressed the architecture of the hotel and condo pieces differently but kept all of the rooftops low in response to views from the Brooklyn Heights Promenade.

Marvel Architects wrapped the floors of the hotel in a glass curtain wall, where the rooms (interior design is by INC Architecture & Design) are graced with sliding glass walls behind glass guardrails, and elevations facing south and west feature metal-grille sunshades. The rooftop bar and pool are popular warm-weather spots, while the double-height lobby and adjacent restaurant and café are frequented year-round. An architectural highlight is the wood-lined portal, which juts out as a folded canopy on Furman Street and draws people through to the park.

Landscape architect Michael Van Valkenburgh designed the rooftop and adjoining landscape for 1 Hotel, blurring the boundary between hotel and park.

Walk through the portal to the Brooklyn Bridge Park Greenway—a shared walkway/bike path—turn left and then ascend the stairs to Squibb Bridge, stopping at the midpoint of the bridge over Furman Street.

(D3) Squibb Bridge
HNTB/ARUP, 2013/2017

The Brooklyn Heights Promenade, perched above the double-decker Brooklyn-Queens Expressway (BQE), is a remarkable piece of mid-twentieth-century urban design now matched by the Brooklyn Bridge Park below it. Connecting the two is the pedestrian Squibb Bridge, which spans from Squibb Park, located a couple blocks from the Promenade's northern tip, to the edge of Pier 1. Instead of a straight run, the bridge bends a few times to create enough length (about 450 feet [41.8 m]) for an accessible slope between Brooklyn Heights and the waterfront, and to fit itself between two halves of Pierhouse. The zigzag path fits well with HNTB engineer Ted Zoli's idea of replicating the feeling—bounce and all—of traversing elevated walkways in state parks. The intentional bounce was accommodated by an inverted suspension system, with black locust timbers and catenary cable supports below the walking surface.

With the bounce came an unintended sway, which led the Brooklyn Bridge Park Corporation to close it (for three years, ultimately) and hire Arup to stabilize the structure. Their fixes—cable clamps, bolts, and tuned mass dampers—are practically invisible, but so is the bounce, which is noticeable when forcefully jumping on its surface.

(J) Pierhouse

MARVEL ARCHITECTS, 2017 – 90 FURMAN STREET

Just as Squibb Bridge zigzags in plan, so do the two halves of Pierhouse, the Toll Brothers's development with more than one hundred condos—all with views over BBP to Lower Manhattan. Marvel Architects designed Pierhouse as a series of stacked and interlocked townhouses. In turn, with entirely duplex units, the need for corridors on every floor disappeared. The single-loaded corridors that do exist are visible north of the bridge as glazed bands set into the façade of brownstone-like composite-metal panels. The light-colored ends of the two halves of Pierhouse hint at the west side of the buildings.

Walk back to the west end of Squibb Bridge, take the ramp under the bridge (noting its structural underside) and continue to the Greenway to see Pierhouse's west side.

While small windows punctuate the "city" side of Pierhouse, expansive glass walls face the park. Though complex, the organization of the duplexes on this side is clear. Setbacks with planted terraces and parallel walls in limestone articulate the mix of units. Generous plantings, also by Michael Van Valkenburgh, screen the lower units from the people crossing the bridge and walking the Greenway connecting Pier 1 to the higher-numbered piers farther south.

D4

Walk up the Greenway a few steps, turn left and walk up the stairs. Where it meets another path, turn right and follow the path around the lawn until a three-pronged fork; take the left path and stay right to the Granite Prospect.

 ## Pier 1

MVVA, 2010

The first section of Brooklyn Bridge Park to be completed was also its largest, at nearly ten acres (4 ha). Serving as one of the main entries to the park, at the end of Old Fulton Street, Pier 1 has concessions, a playground, and a riverfront promenade with panoramic views of Brooklyn Bridge and Lower Manhattan. But it also has lawns, a kayak launch, water gardens (which we cut through and are part of BBP's system of rainwater collection), and planted areas for those who venture farther into the landscape. The steps that form the Granite Prospect indicate the design of Pier 1 embraces views of Lower Manhattan, but it is also about topography—artificial contours built atop the substantial structure of the old pier.

Walk down the steps to the promenade, left to the corner of Pier 1, then left again. After descending the stairs toward the Greenway, turn right and walk along the curving path past the salt marsh and pier posts. Walk south along the Greenway past the recreational Pier 2 to the Granite Terrace of Pier 3.

 ## Pier 3 Greenway & Berm

MVVA, 2018

This section of the park is layered by three distinct features visible from this terrace. Jutting into the water is the old pier (under construction at the time of writing) covered by an undulating lawn, groves of trees and shrubs, a labyrinth garden, and a multipurpose hardscape at its tip. In the middle is the Greenway Terrace, where two lawns and a terrace covered with salvaged granite invite people to sit down and take in the views. This goes hand in hand with the park's broad parti: active uses are situated on the piers, while more passive enjoyment of the park is located inland, or upland. The laid-back atmosphere here is enabled by the third layer: the planted berm—or "Sound Attenuating Hill"—that significantly cuts down on the sounds of traffic coming from the BQE and Furman Street.

Walk south along the Greenway, past the Pier 4 Beach and its Bird Island to the small boathouse.

(K) Brooklyn Bridge Park Boathouse

ARCHITECTURE RESEARCH OFFICE (ARO), 2017

For some years, the uplands east of Pier 5 and the Marina were home to Smorgasburg, Brooklyn's popular weekly haven for foodies. Although Picnic Peninsula allows park-goers to barbecue along the water's edge, the throngs of vendors and hungry people gave way to lawns, seating, a snaking landscaped berm, and two buildings designed by ARO. The first, the BBP Boathouse, sits close to the water on a riprap, while the second, BBP's Maintenance and Operations Building, is located along Furman Street, hidden behind the berm. Run by the nonprofit Brooklyn Bridge Park Boathouse, the two-story building has kayak storage in its open-air ground floor, with restrooms and a multipurpose room upstairs. Metal grilles wrap the whole building, making it appear porous and letting it glow in the evening hours. Most interesting is the building's rock backdrop, which is also the tip of the snaking berm.

Walk south along the Greenway until the intersecting path just past the concessions building.

The last development parcel to be built is just east of Pier 6 and south of One Brooklyn Bridge Park (a warehouse converted to condos in 2008). Under construction at the time of this writing, the 16- and 30-story residential buildings were designed by ODA for RAL Development and Oliver's Realty Group—meaning the MVVA park is bookended by Eran Chen's architecture.

Pier 6

MVVA, 2010

When Brooklyn Bridge Park was inaugurated in 2010, the
completion of Pier 1 was accompanied by one other area at
a bit of a remove: the uplands portion of Pier 6. With just
a crude path initially connecting them, the walk to Pier 6 was
(and is) worth the trip; while Pier 1 has a playground, the
latter has *four*—none of them close to the traditional types
found across the city. South of the walkway connecting
the park to Atlantic Avenue is Swing Valley, with a multitude
of swing sets in a rolling landscape. North of the walkway
are Water Lab, complete with a field of water jets and
an Archimedes' screw; Sandbox Village, billed as "possibly"
the largest sandbox in NYC; and Slide Mountain, where
not only slides, but also climbing equipment are tucked
amongst stands of bamboo.

Pier 6 proper has a restaurant with roof terrace, sand
volleyball courts, lawns, a flower field, and viewing
platform (designed by Bjarke Ingels) in progress at its far
corner. Like some of the other piers that have been reused
for recreational purposes, steel framing at the perimeter
walkway reminds visitors of the site's industrial past.
Though subtle, the repurposed structure literally frames
the twenty-first-century landscape built atop last
century's industry.

*End of tour. Want to see more landscapes in the area?
Walk out to Atlantic Avenue, then left on Hicks Street,
and another left on Remsen Street to walk the
Brooklyn Heights Promenade (Clarke & Rapuano, 1951).
Or take the ferry (summer weekends only) from Pier 6
to Governors Island to see the Hills (West 8 et al., 2016)
at the southern tip of the island.*

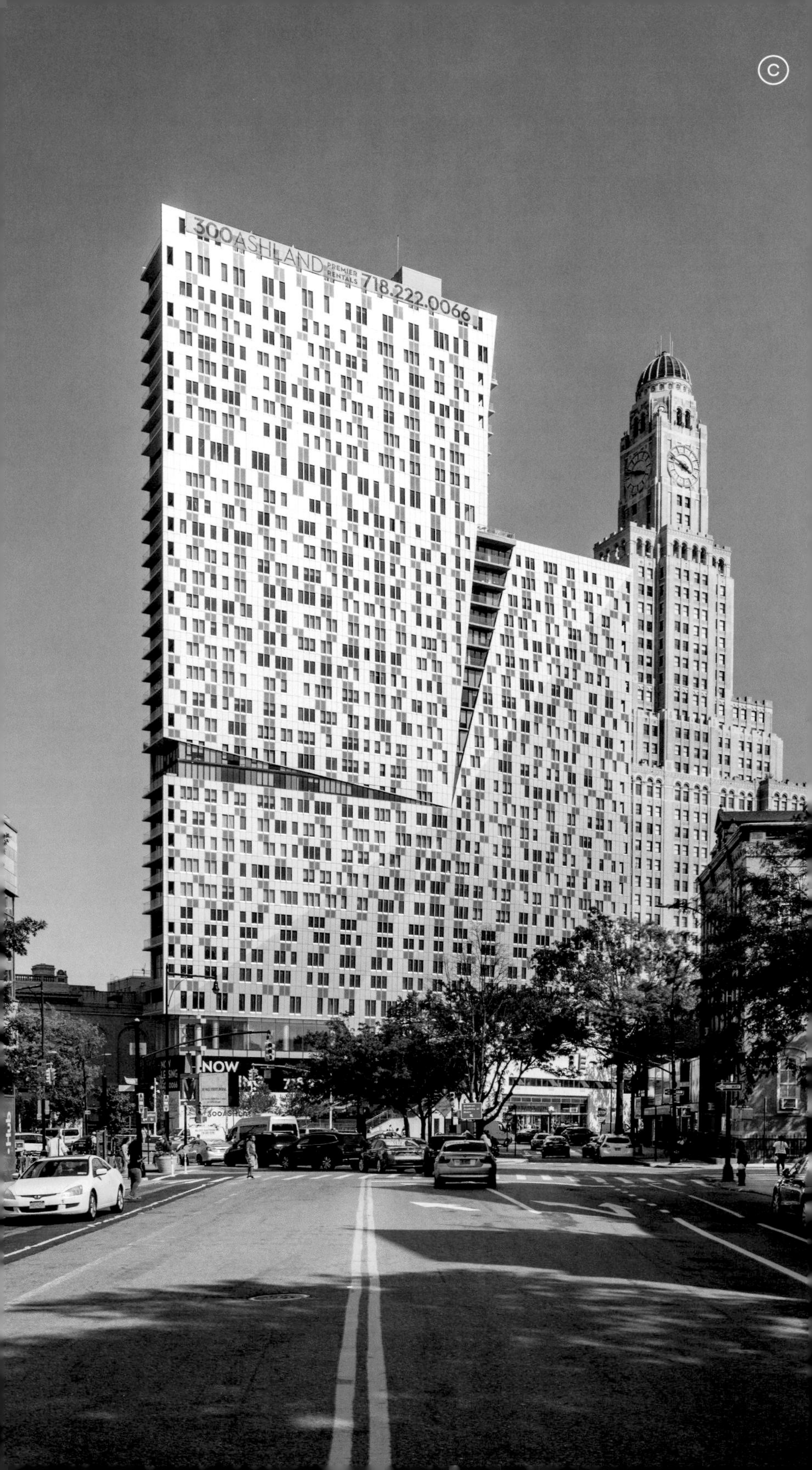
300ASHLAND
PREMIER RENTALS
718.222.0066

9

G Train Tour
of Brooklyn

3.5 MILES / 5.6 KM PLUS SUBWAY RIDES

⟩ *This tour starts at 160 Schermerhorn Street and ends
at the Williamsburg waterfront. It involves two subway rides
so having fare before starting the tour is recommended.*

My earliest architecture tours were organized through the
92nd Street Y's Tribeca location, which shuttered in 2013.
Accordingly, my tours focused in and near downtown, such as
the High Line [TOUR 3] and the Bowery [TOUR 4]. To expand
beyond the confines of Manhattan's southern tip, I decided to
leap over the East River to Brooklyn. Yet without a density of
notable contemporary buildings comparable to the Manhattan
tours, it became necessary to hit a few neighborhoods, getting
on and off the subway to do so. The G Train, which connects
Brooklyn and Queens, made the most sense, since it's the only
non-shuttle service that doesn't enter Manhattan. In turn,
this tour has three parts: it starts on the edge of Downtown
and Boerum Hill before moving to Fort Greene, then heads
to Clinton Hill, and ends up in North Williamsburg.

Depending on how long you've been standing on the
sidewalk at 160 Schermerhorn Street, you may have felt a rumble
beneath your feet. Typically, the roll of subway cars is not felt
on the sidewalk since the majority of subway lines built with the
cut-and-cover method (digging up the street, laying the tracks,
and covering them over) locate the tracks beneath the street
and the platforms beneath the sidewalk. But this stretch of the
G line, which meets up with the A/C lines one block to the east
at Hoyt–Schermerhorn, is different: its six sets of tracks are side
by side rather than stacked, making them wider than the street.
Due to the cut-and-cover method, buildings along the south side
of Schermerhorn were demolished starting in the late 1920s.
Despite later attempts to develop them, the lots served as parking
lots all the way into this century. One of the first buildings that
finally rose along this stretch of Schermerhorn is the one you're
standing in front of.

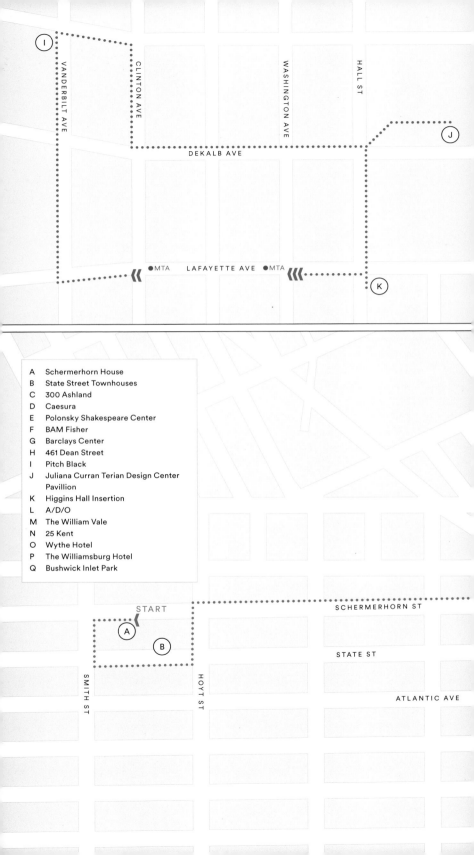

A   Schermerhorn House
B   State Street Townhouses
C   300 Ashland
D   Caesura
E   Polonsky Shakespeare Center
F   BAM Fisher
G   Barclays Center
H   461 Dean Street
I   Pitch Black
J   Juliana Curran Terian Design Center
    Pavillion
K   Higgins Hall Insertion
L   A/D/O
M   The William Vale
N   25 Kent
O   Wythe Hotel
P   The Williamsburg Hotel
Q   Bushwick Inlet Park

VANDERBILT AVE
CLINTON AVE
WASHINGTON AVE
HALL ST
DEKALB AVE
MTA   LAFAYETTE AVE   MTA
SMITH ST
HOYT ST
START
SCHERMERHORN ST
STATE ST
ATLANTIC AVE

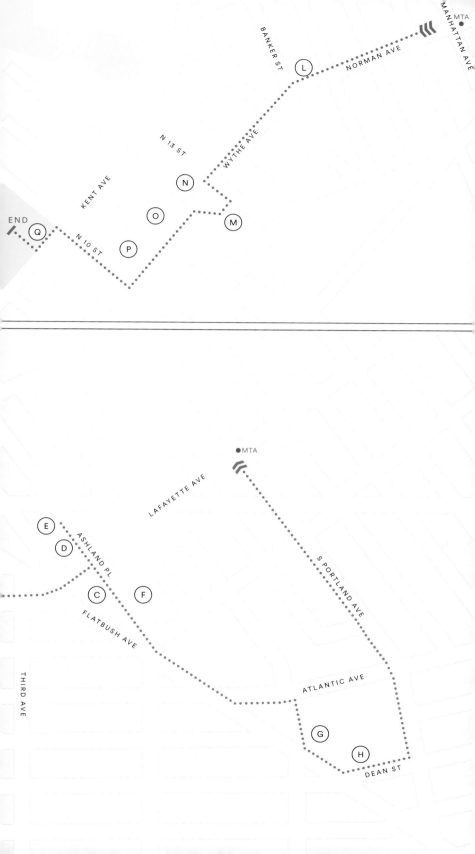

A   Schermerhorn House

ENNEAD ARCHITECTS, 2009 – 160 SCHERMERHORN STREET

Beneath both sidewalk level and the front of this building, the G line and A/C lines crisscross. The 11-story building cantilevers over the MTA tunnels via four two-story-tall trusses (one is visible inside the lobby) that transfer gravity loads to the rear, where 100 caissons more than 50 feet (15.2 m) deep anchor the building to the earth. Upstairs are more than 200 units of supportive housing for the client, Breaking Ground (Common Ground at the time of completion). These micro-units—housing formerly homeless individuals, people living with HIV/AIDS, and low-income workers in the theater industry—can be read on the north façade as vertical stripes alternating between translucent channel glass and clear, operable windows. The horizontal bands of channel glass bathe the residences in soft light, while the windows provide the natural ventilation required by building code. To realize this project, Breaking Ground received the land from the developer of the 23 townhouses on the same block. Providing a lower-income yin to the townhouses' market-rate yang, Schermerhorn House also acts as a hinge between the tall buildings of Downtown Brooklyn and the traditional, low-scale fabric of Boerum Hill.

Walk west to Smith Street, turn left and cross State Street, turn left again and walk to the middle of the block, opposite a handful of old brownstones.

B   State Street Townhouses

ROGERS MARVEL ARCHITECTS, 2006/2013

State Street defines the northern edge of Boerum Hill, a neighborhood that, along with Brooklyn Heights, Carroll Gardens, Cobble Hill, Fort Greene, and Park Slope, comprises "Brownstone Brooklyn." These neighborhoods contain some of the city's most coveted residential building stock, with numerous swaths of them turned into landmark districts. Although this block sits outside of the Boerum Hill Historic District, it contains buildings on the National Register of Historic Places, such as the Italianate townhouses across the street. Flanking them are two groups of 4-story townhouses—14 on the left and 9 on the right—developed by Hamlin Ventures and Time Equities. The two phases of the multimillion-dollar townhouses were separated by the economic crash and therefore completed seven years apart. Nevertheless, together they "complete" the block, as Rogers Marvel Architects (now Rogers Partners and Marvel Architects) strove to do, designing buildings with rooflines that match the historic neighbors. Ten of the 14 townhouses, completed in 2006, have

orange-brick fronts separated from their neighbors by subtle dark-brick reveals and broken up by four townhouses with below-grade entries and roof terraces framed by large openings. Details on the 9 townhouses, completed in 2013, are different: dark-steel window frames, slightly angled brick fronts, copper accents, and a copper-clad corner townhouse that stands out as a singular statement.

Continue east to Hoyt Street, turn left to Schermerhorn Street, turn right and head east three blocks to the small triangle where Schermerhorn meets Flatbush Avenue.

(C) 300 Ashland

TEN ARQUITECTOS, 2017 – 300 ASHLAND PLACE

Fifteen years before the completion of this 379-unit rental development that will include retail, dance studios for 651 Arts, a new home for the Museum of Contemporary African Diasporan Arts, movie theaters for the Brooklyn Academy of Music (BAM), and a new branch of the Brooklyn Public Library, architect Enrique Norten won a competition for a much smaller project on the same site: the Brooklyn Visual and Performing Arts Library. The earlier design filled a portion of the pencil-tip-shaped site with a V-shaped building that opened toward steps and a plaza on the northern, wider end of the block. The new mixed-use building for Two Trees Management retains that open-space parti with a slender 35-story stepped tower along the site's eastern edge on Ashland Place, a tapered podium filling the southern tip and western edge along

Flatbush Avenue, and a terraced plaza designed by James Corner Field Operations toward Lafayette Avenue on the north. The expansive metal-and-glass elevations facing east and west give the project its strongest presence within Brooklyn's increasingly dense and tall Downtown. Staggered windows, two shades of gray, and triangular cuts give the tower a sculptural presence, as if it were pleated and sliced. Although the narrow, slablike design calls attention to itself, the ten-story stepping of the tower defers to its neighboring landmark: Williamsburgh Savings Bank Building (now One Hanson Place), Brooklyn's tallest building from 1929 until 2010.

300 Ashland is the largest of a handful of projects spearheaded by the New York City Economic Development Corporation as part of the Downtown Brooklyn Cultural District (formerly BAM Cultural District). Four of the five projects are discussed here; the fifth, Thomas Leeser's transformation of an old vaudeville theater into BRIC Arts, is located at Fulton Street and Rockwell Place. The creation of the district aimed to foster Fort Greene as a cultural hub and accompanied a larger rezoning that led to a boom in towers along Flatbush Avenue.

Cross Flatbush at Lafayette, beneath which the G Train runs, and walk to Ashland Place.

(D) Caesura

DATTNER ARCHITECTS AND BERNHEIMER ARCHITECTURE, 2018 – 280 ASHLAND PLACE

Sitting on a formerly empty, city-owned lot that afforded a view of the lively mural on the side of the Mark Morris Dance Center, Caesura is the result of a 2013 RFP (Request for Proposal) for the last development lot in the Downtown Brooklyn Cultural District. The impetus for the building is the 49 permanently affordable units (out of 123 total rentals) developed by Jonathan Rose, though it also includes a new home for the Center for Fiction and additional space for Mark Morris. The 12-story building is broken down through massing and materials: the first through a corner setback at the sixth floor and the second in the color of the terracotta rainscreen panels at the base and bricks at the top.

Cross Lafayette and walk to the plaza halfway up the block.

(E) Polonsky Shakespeare Center

H3 HARDY COLLABORATION ARCHITECTURE, 2013 – 262 ASHLAND PLACE

When completed in 2013 as the first permanent home of the Theatre for a New Audience (TFANA, est. 1979), the Polonsky Shakespeare Center became the first theater built in New York

City for classic drama since the Vivian Beaumont Theater at Lincoln Center in the 1960s. Another link between the two projects is architect Hugh Hardy, who added the Claire Tow Theater [6H] atop the Beaumont and designed a 299-seat theater for TFANA in the Downtown Brooklyn Cultural District. The gunmetal gray sidewalls hint at the black-box theater inside, which is accompanied by studio and support spaces. Fronting the building and its sizable plaza (designed by Ken Smith Workshop) is a curtain wall suspended from a large beam hidden at the roof. Behind the glass is the second-floor lobby that is cantilevered over the entrance and turns theatergoers into an urban spectacle. Sitting on a block surrounded by subway lines, much of the building's success as a dramatic venue depends on hidden features: the backstage and the theater are treated as separate structures (separated by a 2-inch [5 cm] gap), with the theater sitting on 8-inch-thick (20 cm), steel-reinforced rubber pads that keep trains from disturbing the modern-day renditions of Shakespeare's plays.

Backtrack to and cross Lafayette, then stop halfway down the block.

F BAM Fisher

H3 HARDY COLLABORATION ARCHITECTURE, 2012 – 321 ASHLAND PLACE

This block of Ashland Place is crowded with Brooklyn Academy of Music (BAM) facilities: the side of its main Peter Jay Sharp Building, the four volumes cantilevering from 300 Ashland that house BAM's cinemas, and the BAM Fisher, which was built to celebrate the institution's 150th anniversary and yet another part of the Downtown Brooklyn Cultural District. BAM Fisher is a six-story addition to a two-story Salvation Army building from 1928; the former features 100-seat and 250-seat venues for intimate performances, classrooms, offices, as well as support spaces, while the latter serves as the lobby. The addition's exterior is clad in orange bricks that make it fit well with the 1928 building. Two windows hint at the functions inside, while a trellis visible at the roof does the same with the parties taking place on the landscaped roof terrace.

Continue south along Ashland Place as it becomes Flatbush Avenue until you cross Atlantic Avenue to reach the triangular plaza.

G Barclays Center

SHOP ARCHITECTS, 2012 – 620 ATLANTIC AVENUE

Barclays Center anchors the west end of the massive Pacific Park Brooklyn development, a project so large and complex as to warrant its own book—someday, if and when it ever wraps up. A quick and dirty history of what started as Atlantic Yards (the name changed when China's Greenland Holdings Group bought a majority of the project in 2013) goes back at least to the mid-1990s, when developer Bruce Ratner of Forest City Ratner built Atlantic Center with 400,000 square feet (37,161 sq m) of big-box retail on Atlantic one block east of Flatbush. About ten years later he added the same amount of retail as an indoor mall across the street, linking them by a bridge, topping it with an office tower, and dubbing it Atlantic Terminal (it sits over a Long Island Rail Road [LIRR] terminal). Ratner's move toward larger and more complicated projects continued unabated with Atlantic Yards' nearly $5 billion plan for 17 towers (office and residential), retail, and a sports arena built over LIRR's rail yards just across the street from his two earlier projects. Frank Gehry's master plan for the nearly 7-million-square-foot (650,321 sq m) project was unveiled in late 2003, around the time that work on Atlantic Terminal wrapped up.

Even with *New York Times* architecture critic Herbert Muschamp praising the Gehry project, opposition followed quickly after its unveiling, due to the scale of the project but also the need for eminent domain to acquire some blocks adjacent to the rail yards to enlarge the plan's footprint beyond that of the yards. It wasn't until late 2009 that any barriers to eminent domain were eliminated, but by then the project was "on life support" according to the *New York Times*; Gehry was out of the picture and SHoP Architects was brought on board to get the arena built in just one year. Since Gehry's plan used the structure of four towers at the development's western end to support the arena, it was impossible to move forward with just the arena—the one element that could advance during the recession. Facing a deadline with banks, Ratner brought on Ellerbe Becket (now part of AECOM) to design a basic arena based on a field house they realized in Indianapolis. In response to a scathing critique of the arena design in the *New York Times*, SHoP was tasked with covering the building in something distinctive.

Although most of the attention goes to the 12,000 Cor-Ten steel panels wrapping all sides of the arena, the cantilevered oculus and LED screen over the plaza, and the large green roof over the arena (this piece was added in 2015), SHoP's strongest design feature was depressing the arena as low as possible to minimize its height. Visitors to Brooklyn Nets basketball games and other events walk from the plaza and into the arena at the level of the scoreboard and then descend to their seats. With a banding of glass and Cor-Ten steel between sidewalk and roof level on the exterior, the arena appears low-slung, especially as the towers of Pacific Park rise behind it.

Continue along Flatbush Avenue past Barclays Center and turn left on Dean Street.

(H) 461 Dean Street

SHOP ARCHITECTS, 2017

This 32-story tower is the first of three towers with 1,500 residences planned for the south and east edges of Barclays Center. Also known as B2 (based on the approved 14-tower master plan that removed tower B1 from the tip at Flatbush), the tower is notable for being the tallest modular building in the world. Setbacks and colors of the cladding give the impression that B2 is three buildings bundled together.

Given that B2's 930 modules were slated to be erected in only 14 months and completed in 2014, it did not turn out to be the prefab demonstration project it was envisioned to be. Technical problems, cost overruns, and squabbling between Forest City Ratner (FCR) and Skanska—hired to produce the modules at a factory in the Brooklyn Navy Yard that they specially built for the project—dragged the project out for years. In the end, Skanska pulled out of the project, FCR finished it on their own and then sold the modular factory to FullStack Modular, a new company that sees promise in modular construction even though this project didn't reveal any.

Walk east along Dean Street, left on 6th Avenue, which turns into South Portland Avenue on the other side of Atlantic Avenue. Continue north to the Fulton Street subway station at Lafayette Avenue, taking a Queens-bound G Train to Clinton–Washington Avenues. Exit via Clinton, walk west one block to Vanderbilt Avenue, then turn right and walk north.

(I) Pitch Black

ADJAYE ASSOCIATES, 2006 – 208 VANDERBILT AVENUE

The name of the Clinton Hill studio David Adjaye designed for artists James Casebere and Lorna Simpson is apt: the four-story building is covered in dark panels. What might be judged from a distance to be metal is actually polypropylene: insulated panels that appear textured but are smooth to the touch. Light-colored, the panels were silk-screened to give them their "Pitch Black" appearance. They cover the front and the side elevation; the latter is visible thanks to the neighboring Hill Center, whose walkway affords a view of the studio's glassy rear façade.

Continue to Willoughby Avenue, turn right to Clinton Avenue and turn right again.

Clinton Avenue is home to numerous nineteenth-century mansions, and this block notably contains four built by oilman

Charles Pratt. On the west side of the street (now part of St. Joseph's College), is Pratt's own house from 1874. Across the street are three houses he built for three of his sons as wedding gifts. One decade after erecting his mansion, the richest man in Brooklyn founded Pratt Institute, the next stop on this tour.

Walk down to DeKalb Avenue, then turn left to Hall Street/St. James Place, and enter through the corner gate to Pratt Institute's campus.

Charles Pratt founded <u>Pratt Institute</u> in 1887 as a design and engineering college that would be open to everybody regardless of race, gender, and income. The dozen students in the school's first year were hardly an auspicious start, but enrollment grew quickly—to more than 4,000 students just five years later. Around 4,500 students are now enrolled in programs in art and design, architecture, information and library sciences, liberal arts and sciences, and continuing education and professional studies—just about everything but engineering, which the school dropped in 1993 due to low enrollment. Early buildings fronted the streets and avenues, but campus expansion in the 1950s and 60s—combined with urban renewal czar Robert Moses's clearing of many adjacent buildings—led to street closures and an ad hoc quadrangle defined by the backs of those same buildings. Now totaling 25 acres (10 ha), the buildings combine with the landscape and rotating display of sculptures to create a vibrant yet cohesive campus.

Walk past the eighteenth-century cannon, take a slight turn right and walk east.

(J) ## Juliana Curran Terian Design Center Pavilion
HANRAHAN MEYERS, 2007 – 200 WILLOUGHBY AVENUE

Much of the campus's cohesion today can be attributed to Thomas Schutte, Pratt's president from 1993 to 2017. In his first year he took the money saved by closing the School of Engineering to fix up and modernize its late nineteenth- and early twentieth-century buildings and beautify the campus. Schutte added the sculpture park in 1999, the same year Thomas Hanrahan, dean of the School of Architecture, and his partner Victoria Meyers were hired to develop a new campus master plan. Aimed at reinforcing the central campus space, the Juliana Curran Terian Design Center Pavilion is a key component. Internally the pavilion links the older Steuben Hall and Pratt Studios buildings into a single Design Center. A double-height gallery for exhibitions and receptions, covered in glass and dark stainless steel, juts toward the sculpture park, emphasizing the importance of this outdoor space.

*Walk back to the corner gate at DeKalb Avenue and head
south on St. James Place across Lafayette Avenue.*

(K) Higgins Hall Insertion

STEVEN HOLL ARCHITECTS, 2005 – 61 ST. JAMES PLACE

The Pratt Institute School of Architecture sits one block south
of campus, separated by St. James Towers, a large urban renewal
project from the 1960s that Pratt now occupies in part. Called
Higgins Hall, the nineteenth-century buildings were originally
the Adelphi Academy, obtained by Pratt in 1965 and named for
alumnus John Higgins. A four-alarm fire hit in 1996, just as portions
were being renovated by Rogers Marvel Architects (RMA). The
central portion was taken down due to extensive damage, while
the north wing was restored by Ehrenkrantz Eckstut & Kuhn
Architects and the south wing was reconstructed by RMA. Dean
Hanrahan brought in Steven Holl to design a replacement for the
central section.

Holl, working with RMA, designed a lantern-like building that
sits on the foundation of the old building and reuses some of its
brick in the slightly raised forecourt. The majority of the front and
rear façades is covered in translucent channel glass that spans
from floor to floor. Holl matched the insertion to the floor levels
of the north and south wings, expressing their difference through
the horizontal lines on the façades and the so-called "dissonance
zone" where they meet, a composition of clear-glass panes
in various sizes and alignments. Behind this glass are ramps that
connect the offset floors and are illuminated by north-facing

skylights. The various apertures and types of glass bathe the architecture studios in plenty of light, and at night the insertion glows—a beacon in the neighborhood and sign of students pulling all-nighters.

> *Walk west on Lafayette Avenue back to the*
> *Clinton–Washington station, taking the Queens-bound*
> *G Train to Nassau Avenue.*

Greenpoint is a transit desert, served by just one subway line. That it's the G Train—shorter, with only four cars, and running less frequently than other lines—makes this very northwest corner of Brooklyn less trodden by outsiders than its neighbor to the south, Williamsburg.

> *Exit at Norman Avenue, cross Manhattan Avenue and*
> *continue west on Norman Avenue for three blocks.*

(L) A/D/O

NARCHITECTS, 2016 – 29 NORMAN AVENUE

If any name conceals, rather than reveals, its purpose, it's A/D/O. Knowing that the building houses a creative space opened by MINI—and takes its name from the carmaker's early Amalgamated Drawing Office—helps just a little. One has to walk inside the building, through the glass storefront that's been cut at an angle into the former one-story warehouse, to see the hive of activity that is A/D/O.

Before stepping inside, take a closer look at the brick walls: Eric Bunge and Mimi Hoang of nARCHITECTS "remixed" the existing, graffiti-covered brick walls into what they call

"reconstituted graffiti." This is evident in the strip above the new storefront glass and in old openings that were filled in or received smaller windows or doors than the original. Combined with the intact graffiti, the effect is collage-like, as if A/D/O is stitched together from equal parts old and new.

Inside, on the other side of the "porch" and new storefront, is the publicly accessible area, with a restaurant to the left, a shop to the right, and a seating area straight ahead. The last is highlighted by the "Periscope," a kaleidoscopic skylight with mirrored panels that unites reflected images of the Brooklyn and Manhattan skylines into one—at least when seen from the right angle of repose. People working at the tables in the open space hint at the private spaces that take up most of A/D/O's footprint: member-based work spaces, a start-up accelerator focused on "engineering the city as a service," and a design academy with lectures and seminars.

Exit A/D/O and cross Banker Street to continue south along Wythe Avenue to North 13th Street, turn left, and then right to the pedestrian walkway.

(M) The William Vale

ALBO LIBERIS, 2016 – 111 NORTH 12TH STREET

We are standing beneath the tower visible for much of our walk from the G Train to this edge of Greenpoint and Williamsburg. At 22 stories, the William Vale, developed by Zelig Weiss, is relatively short by New York standards, but it towers above the surrounding manufacturing district to be a new local landmark. The expressed diagonal bracing, intended by architects Yohay Albo and Nicholas Liberis to recall old water towers, aids in this distinction; it also expresses the tower's two main uses: medical office space behind the bracing and a 183-room hotel with wraparound balconies above. The tower straddles the two low-rise structures on either side of the pedestrian walkway: to the west is one-story retail behind concrete columns; to the east is enclosed parking wrapped in wood slats.

(M)

Head up the external stair at the base of the tower to the raised public space on top of the retail podium.

NYC is full of hotels with crowded rooftop bars and terraces. The William Vale is no different, with its own version on the 22nd floor, but it also provides this public space designed by Gunn Landscape Architecture. Rather than sweeping, views are focused on the William Vale's own tower, a convergence of more hotels down Wythe Avenue, and, since 2018, the building across the street.

(N) 25 Kent

HOLLWICH KUSHNER & GENSLER, 2019

While hotels, restaurants, and other hospitality uses are allowable in manufacturing districts, offices require ULURP (Uniform Land Use Review Procedure), an often-lengthy process that many developers shy away from; hence Wythe Avenue is lined with hotels rather than office buildings. 25 Kent, though, is a special case, the first built project in a special "Enhanced Business Area" the city implemented in this swath of North Williamsburg. Heritage Equity Partners, targeting tech companies large and small, developed this full-block project with seven floors of flexible office space and 20 percent of the overall square footage devoted to light manufacturing. The ziggurat-like building uses brick to provide a quasi-industrial aesthetic, while a glazed middle section sets a contrast and caps a retail-lined walkway that will connect Wythe Avenue with the expanded Bushwick Inlet Park [Q]—whenever that is completed.

Go down the stair that leads to Wythe Avenue and walk south to North 11th Street.

(O) Wythe Hotel

MORRIS ADJMI ARCHITECTS, 2012 – 80 WYTHE AVENUE

This is the one that started it all. Williamsburg's already intense gentrification went next level with this 72-room hotel that brought tourists to the neighborhood and Manhattanites to its rooftop bar. Under developer Jed Walentas (Two Trees) and restaurateur/hotelier Andrew Tarlow, architect Morris Adjmi transformed an old textile factory into *the* place to be. Its success could hardly be attributed exclusively to the architecture, but the mix of old and new—the renovated five-story factory and four-story glass-walled addition—works as a respectful transformation that should be commended. To accommodate the new floors on top and stay within the allowable zoning, the westernmost bay of the factory was cut off and its exposed end was covered with a new curtain wall that matches the addition. Lastly, the "HOTEL" sign and

P

custom entry door draw attention to the distinctive inset corner, supposedly made to lift and lower barrels in its pre-hotel days.

⋮ *Walk one block south along Wythe Avenue.*

P

The Williamsburg Hotel

MICHAELIS BOYD ASSOCIATES, 2017 – 96 WYTHE AVENUE

Of the North Williamsburg hotels following on the heels of Wythe Hotel's success, the Williamsburg Hotel is the oddest architecturally. With a slender east-west plan, continuous balconies facing north, a façade of Cor-Ten steel on the south, an expanse of solid brick spelling out the name of the hotel, and an oversize water tank at the corner, the 150-room hotel looks like an assemblage of buildings. In fact, it is all of a piece, a new building dreamt up by the UK firm of Alex Michaelis and Tim Boyd for Heritage Equity Partners. Amenities are in abundance: a sunken terrace on Wythe; an adjacent, cellar-level bar; a "clandestine" bar entered from North 10th Street; a huge ballroom at the west end of the building; and inside that water tank? A bar with charred-timber and steel-panel walls, colored glass, and glass flooring at the perimeter giving views to the street below.

Walk west on North 10th Street to Kent Avenue then left one block.

(Q) Bushwick Inlet Park

KISS + CATHCART & STARR WHITEHOUSE, 2013

In 2005, New York's Department of City Planning approved a major rezoning of a two-mile (3.2 km) stretch of the East River waterfront in Williamsburg and Greenpoint, spanning from North 3rd Street to just shy of the Pulaski Bridge. Nearly 200 blocks changed from manufacturing to residential districts, paving the way for the construction of residential towers with views of the Manhattan skyline. An important ingredient in the rezoning was open space, with much of it focused on a seven-block stretch between North 7th Street and the small Bushwick Inlet at North 14th Street. To date, only half of the proposed parkland has been constructed, made up of the seven-acre (2.8 ha) East River State Park, and the first phase of the Bushwick Inlet Park. Intended to encompass 27 acres (11 ha), the first phase consists of just over six acres (2.4 ha); the remaining land to the north, occupied by old warehouses and refineries, wasn't acquired by the city until November 2016.

The Bushwick Inlet Park that opened in 2013 is made up of three main elements: a building with community and maintenance facilities along Kent Avenue, an athletic field with artificial turf in the middle, and a wetland basin at the river's edge.

Walk toward the river but then follow the zigzagging path to the top of the building.

Kiss + Cathcart designed the sloped building that is capped by a PV (photovoltaic) array, while Starr Whitehouse was responsible for the landscape. Although distinct, the project's three parts define a continuous landscape, with grass even covering the roof of the building. Stormwater management also unites these parts: rainwater hitting paved surfaces is collected for irrigation, while rainwater in other parts either percolates into the ground or enters the river via a tidal wetland; none of the rain hitting the site enters the city's combined sewer system.

End of tour. Want to continue to Tour 10? Walk south to North 6th Street, then right to take the East River ferry to the East 34th Street stop in Manhattan.

10 East River by Ferry

1.75 MILES / 2.8 KM PLUS FERRY RIDES

⟩ *This tour starts at the northwest corner of First Avenue and 35th Street in Manhattan, at the entrance to St. Vartan Park and ends on Roosevelt Island. It involves two short ferry rides connecting three short walks.*

For most of its existence, the main spine of New York City has been up the center of the island of Manhattan. This course of development made sense, given the industrial piers along the Hudson and East Rivers. But in this century, with Brooklyn taking over as the epicenter of culture, Queens named the best place to visit (by Lonely Planet) in 2015, miles of waterfront in Brooklyn and Queens being redeveloped for residential use and ferries serving those developments, the center of gravity is shifting to the East River. Mayor Bloomberg launched East River Ferry Service in 2011, the same year the city released *Vision 2020: New York City Comprehensive Waterfront Plan*, which aimed to enliven the waterfront and improve the public's access to it. By 2018, waterfront development under Mayor de Blasio continued, while the renamed NYC Ferry was serving more than 1.4 million people per year, from the Rockaways to the Bronx. Ferries serve as our means of visiting projects in Manhattan, Queens, and Roosevelt Island (technically part of Manhattan) on both sides of—*and in*—the East River.

(A) American Copper Buildings

SHOP ARCHITECTS, 2017 – 626 FIRST AVENUE

Developers building "luxury rentals" in Manhattan is to be expected, as is building along the waterfront and providing some affordable units through the Inclusionary Housing Program in order to gain tax breaks. But building a sky-bridge between two residential towers is unexpected, something more akin to a hospital complex. Each of the other developments in the collaboration of JDS Development and SHoP Architects— 111 West 57th Street [5E] and 9 DeKalb in Brooklyn—are supertall towers that make statements through height and slenderness.

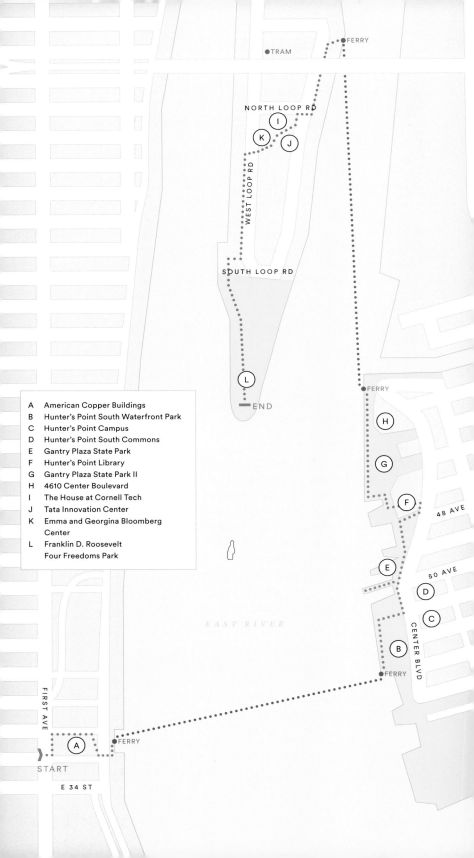

TRAM
FERRY

NORTH LOOP RD

I
K J

WEST LOOP RD

SOUTH LOOP RD

FERRY

L
END

A American Copper Buildings
B Hunter's Point South Waterfront Park
C Hunter's Point Campus
D Hunter's Point South Commons
E Gantry Plaza State Park
F Hunter's Point Library
G Gantry Plaza State Park II
H 4610 Center Boulevard
I The House at Cornell Tech
J Tata Innovation Center
K Emma and Georgina Bloomberg
   Center
L Franklin D. Roosevelt
   Four Freedoms Park

H

G

F

48 AVE

E

50 AVE

D

C

EAST RIVER

CENTER BLVD

B

FERRY

FIRST AVE

FERRY

A

START

E 34 ST

Here, the team effectively took one tower and split it and its 761 units into two "dancing" towers of 41 and 48 stories, connecting them with a two-story sky bridge at levels 28 and 29. Sitting astride the six-story River School/P.S. 281 (Mitchell Giurgola Architects, 2013), the twin-ish towers are said to be dancing because each bends toward the other at the level of the 100-foot-long (30 m) sky bridge, shortening the span versus perfectly orthogonal masses.

Cross First Avenue, walk north to 36th Street, and then turn right and walk into the plaza between the towers.

The slight bends of each tower are more noticeable from this open space: the taller west tower leans toward the East River at the lower half and then back to the west on the upper floors, while the shorter east tower leans north and then south. That the towers have the same orientation—narrow, all-glass ends facing east and west, and windows set into copper skins on the north-south façades—means they "dance" distinctly. It also means the copper panels should patina at different rates over time, depending on their orientation and overhang. The diagonal insertion of the sky bridge, complete with a lap pool on the lower level and a lounge upstairs, makes the assemblage a bit jarring, especially seen from the plaza.

Designed by SCAPE Landscape Architecture, the plaza is meant to serve social and ecological functions. Sitting above a parking structure, the plaza provides seating for the public, arranged about a large fountain meant to cut down on the traffic noise of neighboring FDR Drive. The water feature hints at the invisible measures that collect stormwater runoff, store water during heavy rains, and protect the building in the event of coastal flooding. Post-Hurricane Sandy features are not limited to the plaza, though; the west tower is topped by emergency generators—as much an amenity in our age of climate change as the pool and spa atop the east tower.

Walk down to 35th Street and cross FDR Drive to the East 34th Street ferry stop (Kennedy & Violich Architecture, 2012). Take a ferry on the East River route one stop to Hunters Point South.

(B) ## Hunter's Point South Waterfront Park
ARUP, THOMAS BALSLEY ASSOCIATES & WEISS/MANFREDI, 2013

Ferry passengers disembark at the southern end of the first phase of Hunter's Point South Waterfront Park, next to a pavilion with a dramatically swooping canopy and an urban beach—a sandbox the size of a city playground. The park's second phase extends to the south and is anchored by its own dramatic feature: an overlook cantilevered over wetlands. Totaling 10 acres (4 ha), the park mixes active and passive uses and serves as the front yard for the 30-acre (12 ha) Hunter's Point South development, which will build nearly 5,000 housing units (60 percent of them affordable) across seven parcels from 50th Avenue down to Newtown Creek. The whole is the transformation of a formerly industrial strip of waterfront in Long Island City, Queens, into a residential neighborhood envisioned at one time as housing for athletes in New York City's failed 2012 Olympics bid. Engineering firm Arup was in charge of infrastructure for both park and development, while landscape architect Thomas Balsley (now SWA/Balsley) and multidisciplinary firm Weiss/Manfredi collaborated on the park design. Since the second phase was under construction at the time of this writing, the walking route of this tour focuses on phase one.

Walk to the corner of the pier just beyond the pavilion's canopy.

One could argue that the pleated canopy supported by leaning columns is excessive or a self-conscious attempt at making an architectural statement. But the steel structure makes perfect sense and serves numerous purposes. First, in a landscape soon to be surrounded by numerous high rises, the structure gives the park a highly visible landmark, a point of interest that draws people—be it from land or water. Second, it shelters the tables and chairs served by the café in the enclosed portion of the

building. Third, it's infrastructural, supporting photovoltaic (PV) panels and channeling rainwater to its lower, western tip for the park's irrigation.

⋮ *Walk along the railing to the northern tip of the pier.*

The shape of the integral canopy and building, which houses restrooms and park facilities as well as the café, follows the large oval, itself planted partly in grass and covered in artificial turf. Offering a free canvas for play, the oval serves an ecological purpose: it receives floodwaters and then slowly releases the water back into the river after subsiding. The system was put to the test in 2012 during Hurricane Sandy, when the park was under construction; it succeeded in accommodating the storm's 4-foot (1.2 m) surge.

⋮ *Walk north past the playground and then right between it*
⋮ *and the dog run to the benches just shy of Center Boulevard.*

The first phase of Hunter's Point South Waterfront Park is the active portion, with the second phase geared more to such passive activities as strolling. It makes sense that the oval and basketball courts are located across the street from a school.

(C) ## Hunter's Point Campus
FXFOWLE, 2013 – 1-50 51ST AVENUE

Although it looks like one school, this five-story building cloaked in dark, iron-spot brick houses more than 1,000 students in three public schools: a middle school, a special needs school, and a high school, the Academy for Careers in Television & Film. In the design by FXFOWLE (now FXCollaborative), the large windows set into the brick walls signal the various classrooms, but a couple of large spaces shared by all the schools are visible: the gymnasium sits behind translucent wall panels at the base; and the cafeteria, fronted by a sizable terrace overlooking Manhattan, tops the building. (Not visible but sitting between the two in the middle of the L-shaped plan is the auditorium.) The architects dealt with some tricky site conditions, particularly the Midtown Tunnel clipping the southern end of the site, accommodated by angling the south façade relative to the street.

(D) ## Hunter's Point South Commons
SHOP ARCHITECTS, 2015 – 1-50 50TH AVENUE

Hunter's Point South Commons and Hunter's Point South Living, the tower next to Hunter's Point Campus, comprise the first phase of the roughly 5,000 apartments coming to this corner of Queens.

Both towers have the same architect and developer (Phipps Houses and Related Companies with Monadnock Construction), but the Commons is more interesting in terms of massing and aesthetics. Occupying a whole city block, the Commons fills the site with a low-rise podium for parking and retail; it has two mid-rise wings on the east and west ends; and it places its 37-story tower on the north. This massing maximizes solar orientation for many of its 619 apartments, creates a sizable buffer between it and Hunters Point South Living, and provides plenty of surfaces for such amenities as a rooftop farm and apiary. The façades' assemblage of reflective glazing and orange louvers and frames makes for an appealing addition to a part of Queens studded with many bland residential towers. But the metal tracks that cover much of the podium are an odd touch; while alluding to the industrial freight that used to move along the waterfront, their position at the base makes them look like a memorial to the Twin Towers.

Walk north along the path and then left out onto the first pier of Gantry Plaza State Park.

(E)   ## Gantry Plaza State Park
THOMAS BALSLEY ASSOCIATES, 1998

Ten years before the High Line [TOUR 3] made it hip to reclaim industrial relics for public space, Thomas Balsley incorporated steel gantries into the design of this state park, in turn cementing its name. The 6-acre (2.4 ha) park opened in 1998, four years after ground broke for Queens West, the 74-acre (30 ha) development planned by Gruzen Samton and Beyer Blinder Belle for the Port Authority and city and state economic development corporations. They tried to create a Queens version of Battery Park City (BPC) [TOUR 1], and the completion of Cesar Pelli's stepped Citylights tower the same year as Gantry Plaza State Park signaled that similarly conservative architecture would be employed. But just as BPC's public spaces improve upon the buildings, the diminutive Gantry Park set a strong precedent for the parks that would be realized north and south of it.

Designed by Balsley with landscape architect Lee Weintraub and Sowinski Sullivan Architects, the park is split into a few parts: four piers, a garden and cove, and a plaza and lawn. The reconstructed piers were detailed for particular uses (fishing, sightseeing, eating, ferrying), though over time these have changed. One that remains intact is the fishing pier we're standing on, complete with a stainless-steel table designed for cleaning fish.

Walk inland and a slight left to the interpretive garden.

If the gantries are like a hit over the head with industrial artifacts, this intimate garden is a gentle nudge. Old railroad tracks are set into gravel paths between native plantings and scattered blocks of granite.

Walk north and cross the curved walkway to Gantry Plaza.

The gantries, which unloaded freight onto river barges in their previous lives, were restored and now serve as historical artifacts reminding residents and visitors of New York's waterfront industry. Signaling "Long Island" from Manhattan, their large and intricate parts are most impressive up close. North of the plaza and the fourth pier is Peninsula Park, the last element completed in Balsley's Gantry Park and its most traditional, with a lawn and some trees rung by walkways jutting into the riprap edges.

(F) Hunter's Point Library

STEVEN HOLL ARCHITECTS, 2019 – 47–40 CENTER BOULEVARD

In May 2015, coinciding with the groundbreaking for this seven-story, 22,000-square-foot (2,043 sq m) branch of Queens Library, an exhibition of drawings and models of Steven Holl's design opened at the nearby SculptureCenter. The Long Island City venue was appropriate for more than proximity, given that no New York City project—except perhaps Holl's own Campbell Sports Center [71]—so earns the label "sculptural." A simple

rectilinear concrete block is carved with amoeba-like openings that defy reason, at least when first seen from the outside. But each angular opening corresponds to one or more of the library's interlocking spaces. The largest opening, visible on the left side of the river-facing elevation, follows the amphitheater-like stacks of the adult reading area, angles back toward the atrium, and reaches straight up to give light and views to the teen reading area. Framed views of the Manhattan skyline from these and other spaces (including a children's reading area, "cybercenter," and roof terrace) are the main reason for these openings—and why Holl stacked the building tall.

Walk to Center Boulevard to see the library from the east.

Another reason the architect built vertically was to create a "reading garden" on the east side of the building. Formed by angling the building relative to the street and embraced by a low building designed simply by Holl for park maintenance, the tapered garden designed by Michael Van Valkenburgh is meant to be a tranquil space shaded by ginkgo trees.

The building and landscape were still under construction at the time of this writing, eight long years after Holl was hired for this library branch. Fairly typical budgetary and political issues held up the project, with the most unfortunate bit of value engineering found on the façade. Instead of aluminum foam covering the concrete, the latter was painted with an aluminum paint meant to give the building a subtle sparkle. Unfortunately, with the grain of the formwork showing on the concrete, the exterior looks like painted plywood. Thankfully, the complex interlocking spaces were retained, enticing people to visit the library—and stay a while.

After exploring the library interior, exit to the west, walk
north, turn left at the playground and follow the water's
edge to the seating where the concrete pavers give way to
wood boardwalk.

(G) Gantry Plaza State Park II

ABEL BAINNSON BUTZ (ABB), 2009/2013

About ten years after Balsley's park was built in front of Queens West's first trio of towers, the second phase of Gantry Plaza State Park opened to the public. Completed entirely by 2013, the park's construction coincided with the development of the second phase of Queens West by TF Cornerstone, spanning from 47th Road to Anable Basin on the land of the old Pepsi bottling plant. TF basically followed the approved master plan from the 1990s in the location of its seven towers, but when ABB was brought

on board for the park they eliminated the street along the waterfront. This freed up more space for the park, which is made up largely of lawn areas but has a playground, a community garden, and walkways both along the water and abutting the private landscapes of the residential towers. The most distinctive feature in the park is the Pepsi-Cola sign that was erected on the roof of the bottling plant in 1940, rebuilt in 1993, and then removed in 2003 after Pepsi sold their facility. The glowing beacon of commerce was moved to its current location in 2009 and designated a landmark in 2016.

Walk north along the water's edge and stop in front of the Pepsi sign.

(H) 4610 Center Boulevard

ARQUITECTONICA, 2014

TF Cornerstone's architect of choice for its half dozen towers was Arquitectonica, the Florida firm of Bernardo Fort-Brescia and Laurinda Spear. Although their flashiness evident in the Westin New York at Times Square (2002) had subsided when they crossed the East River, the duo did manage to move Queens West toward an all-glass palette in line with residential towers elsewhere in the city. Although each project walks the usual line between the developer's needs and those of the residents, only the tower at 4610 Center Boulevard had to contend with a giant neon sign just steps away from it. To accommodate the sign, which sits on a small patch of land Pepsi still owns, the architects receded the first eight floors of the 25-story tower by 12 feet (3.65 m). A staggered

203

grid of balconies adds some noise to the elevation facing south, but the muted west façade with rounded glass corners doesn't compete with the sign—intentionally, making it as much a part of the development as of the area's industrial past.

Walk up to the Long Island City ferry stop and take an Astoria-bound ferry one stop to Roosevelt Island. Walk down East Main Street to the northeast corner of the Cornell Tech campus.

The idea to create an applied sciences and engineering campus on Roosevelt Island first came to light in December 2010, when the Applied Sciences NYC competition launched. Mayor Michael Bloomberg wanted to diversify the city's economy after the recession hit two years earlier; tap into the booming technology, science, and engineering sectors; and lure people away from Silicon Valley. The campus would be located on one of four city-owned sites, including 12 acres (4.85 ha) occupied by the Goldwater Memorial Hospital just south of the Queensboro Bridge.

Home to hog farms, a prison, asylums, hospitals, and apartments over the course of the city's 400-year history, the two-mile-long (3.2 km) island went under the names Manning's Island, Blackwell's Island, and Welfare Island before it was changed to Roosevelt Island in 1973 in honor of Franklin D. Roosevelt. Residential development at the time of the name change focused on the middle of the island, north of the bridge. Goldwater, which opened in 1939, stayed active until the end of December 2013, when its patients were transferred to a hospital at the north end of the island and another in Harlem. Taking its place would be Cornell Tech, a consortium of Cornell University and Technion–Israel Institute of Technology that in December 2011 bested six other institutional teams in the Applied Sciences NYC competition. Less than a year later, Cornell Tech would become a reality, operating out of donated space in Google's Chelsea headquarters, and in September 2017 moving to the newly dedicated campus on Roosevelt Island.

Before the Cornell/Technion team was selected, it hired Skidmore, Owings & Merrill (SOM) to aid in site selection and generate ideas for the master plan. Working with landscape firm James Corner Field Operations, SOM developed five principles: a permeable campus connected to its surroundings; a car-free, pedestrian environment; a synergy between indoor and outdoor spaces; the campus as a microcosm of the city; and holistic sustainability. These principles led to a master plan with diagonally arranged buildings—buildings that would strive for the highest standards of sustainability and be elevated above the 500-year floodplain—oriented about the north-south Tech Walk in the center of campus. The first phase is located at the north edge of campus, closest to the tram, subway, and ferry, and consists of a handful of buildings, three of them described below; the others are an education center and hotel designed by Snøhetta and planned for a 2019 completion. Eventually the three-phase campus will be built out to more than 2 million square feet (185,000 sq m) for 2,000 graduate students in computer science, electrical engineering, and other related degrees.

*Walk onto campus and stop just past the entrance
to the House.*

(1) The House at Cornell Tech

HANDEL ARCHITECTS, 2017 – 1 EAST LOOP ROAD

The House, a 26-story, 352-unit apartment building for students and faculty, can boast of being the tallest Passive House building in the world. Following standards established by Germany's Passivhaus Institut, Passive House buildings aim for energy efficiency and comfort. In a nutshell, Passive House standards reduce energy consumption through a heavily insulated, tightly sealed façade and energy-efficient mechanical equipment. Built with triple-glazed windows and large prefabricated exterior wall panels (to reduce the number of joints and therefore air infiltration), Handel Architects's website describes the House's primarily solid façade as "a super-insulated blanket" over the

units that range from studios to three-bedrooms. The little bit of heating and cooling equipment necessary is placed in small rooms behind the louvered "zipper" that runs from the entrance to the terrace at the top of the building, where residents can nab skyline views over the low-rise campus.

Walk south to the Campus Plaza overlooking the two other phase-one buildings.

(J) Tata Innovation Center

WEISS/MANFREDI, 2017 – 11 EAST LOOP ROAD

On the right is the six-story colocation building initially known as the Bridge then renamed following a donation from Tata Consultancy Services. One third of the LEED Gold building houses students, while the balance is given over to tech businesses. Interaction—bridging—between the two groups is paramount, but the unprecedented program was also the main source of consideration for architects Marion Weiss and Michael Manfredi. They responded with two angular wings containing open-plan studios, labs, and offices astride a central "fissure" behind a south-facing angled glass wall. The stepped atrium and generous circulation of the fissure is geared to the incidental interactions so prized in colleges today. Angles also define the generous cantilevers of each wing, one at the northeast corner and at the southwest; studios with raked seating sit above the angled undersides of these cantilevers. The hefty overhangs are supported by large trusses that are written across the façade in diagonal mullions. Floating atop the building is a canopy that shades the roof terrace and supports PV panels for its net-zero neighbor.

(K) Emma and Georgina Bloomberg Center

MORPHOSIS, 2017 – 2 WEST LOOP ROAD

More than 1,400 PV panels float above the four-story Emma and Georgina Bloomberg Center, named for the children of the former NYC mayor after he donated $100 million. Unlike the Tata Center's solar roof, parts of the canopy atop Bloomberg extends beyond the building's perimeter, an expression of freedom but also of the large area required to achieve net zero (no carbon emissions in building operations) with solar panels. At one point in the design process, a continuous PV array uniting the two buildings across the plaza was considered, but the end result maintains the architectural integrity of each building, even as they share resources. Bloomberg Center has other features that push it toward net zero (e.g., geothermal wells and smart building technology), but those are invisible.

Besides the solar canopy, the building's most attention-getting architectural feature is its primarily opaque façade, a highly insulated rainscreen wall system covered in greenish aluminum panels with two-inch (5 cm) circular tabs—337,500 of them—punched at different angles. Done in collaboration with students from Cornell and MIT, each tab corresponds to a single pixel of images enlarged onto the façades: the Manhattan skyline on the west and the Ithaca Gorges on the east. Surfaces on the interior of the building are also canvases for artistic images, such as Michael Riedel's textual *Cornell Tech Mag* that covers the acoustical ceiling tiles in the public cafeteria.

Walk onto the lobby of Tata Center to get a peek of the atrium, then walk across to and through the lobby and café of Bloomberg Center. Walk south on West Loop Road through Southpoint Park (Wallace Roberts & Todd, 2011), past the landmarked ruins of Smallpox Hospital, and through the gate to the base of the FDR memorial's steps.

(L) Franklin D. Roosevelt Four Freedoms Park

LOUIS I. KAHN, 2012 – 1 FDR FOUR FREEDOMS PARK

When FDR Four Freedoms Park opened in October 2012, most media coverage highlighted the decades it took to realize the memorial to the 32nd president of the United States; after all, Louis I. Kahn signed the contract to design the monument on the first day of 1973, the same year the island was renamed in Roosevelt's honor. But all presidential memorials take time. The Washington Monument took fifty-one years to build.

The FDR Memorial in Washington, DC, went through three iterations and took more than forty years of planning before its dedication in 1997. What's more remarkable than time, though, is how closely Kahn's memorial at the southern tip of Roosevelt Island matches the design he finalized shortly before he died in March 1974. Kahn, in collaboration with landscape architect Harriet Pattison, didn't just sketch out the design; he worked it out in detail, with architects David Wisdom and Mitchell Giurgola and landscape architect Lois Sherr Dubin producing working drawings before the city's fiscal crisis hit in 1975 and left the project in limbo. When the project finally moved toward groundbreaking in 2010—seven years after Nathaniel Kahn's documentary, *My Architect*, and five years after an exhibition at the Cooper Union devoted to the project—Mitchell Giurgola served as architect of record and Sherr returned as landscape architect, ensuring continuity. Furthermore, the project's construction was overseen by Gina Pollara, a curator of the 2005 exhibition at Cooper Union.

Walk up the 100-foot-wide (30 m) steps to the head of the lawn.

Although Kahn had not built any memorials in his lifetime, he had considered their design by the time of Four Freedoms. Notably, he was one of 574 entrants in the 1960 competition for the FDR memorial in DC, and in 1972 he wrapped up work on the unbuilt Memorial to the Six Million Jewish Martyrs in Battery Park City. In early 1973 he came to the realization that this FDR memorial should be simply a room and a garden.

The room is about 350 feet (106 m) away, just past the bust of FDR visible at the end of the lawn, the central feature of the garden. Astride it are 120 little leaf lindens—four rows of 30—set into gravel stabilized with resin. The grass and trees taper in plan and slope downward, creating a false perspective that draws us toward the six-foot-tall (1.82 m) bronze bust of Roosevelt based on a Depression-era bust by artist Jo Davidson.

Walk down the lawn or one of the rows of linden trees
and through the forecourt to "the room."

This is the space where Kahn's design finds meaning. The words of Roosevelt's "Four Freedoms" speech, given during his State of the Union address in 1941, are carved into the rear of the granite blocks framing the bronze bust, but the rest of the room is empty, save some benches on the sides and a sunken "ha-ha" at its tip. Granite walls twelve feet (3.6 m) high direct our gaze southward, but narrow, one-inch (2 cm) gaps in the walls push us to the realization that the 36-ton (32.6 tonnes) solid blocks are actually columns—large ones at six feet wide and six feet deep (1.8 x 1.8 m) —that define "the room" in an almost primordial manner. In fact, the blocks weigh more than the maximum load of the bridge entering Roosevelt Island, so the blocks had to be barged to the site, an effort on par with the building of the pyramids. Polished surfaces in the gaps frame views to Manhattan, but they are partial and obscured, unlike the open sky overhead—a rare sight in New York City. From the end of the room, our eyes are drawn to the glass block of the United Nations—its name coined by FDR, a one-time governor of New York State, making the memorial's site almost predetermined. But deeper than any political history is our perspective from a spot *in* the river rather than *next* to the river, as in the waterfront parks created in this century. From here we experience New York as a city of islands and waterways, a natural place that has been tamed through order and geometry over its 400-year existence.

End of tour. For access to Manhattan, walk north out of
Four Freedoms Park and continue along West Loop Road
past the Queensboro Bridge to the Roosevelt Island Tramway,
a unique NYC experience.

20 More
Places to See

To explore contemporary New York City architecture beyond the ten walking tours presented in this book, following are twenty more places worth seeing in person, all completed since 2011, when my first book, *Guide to Contemporary New York City Architecture*, was released.

The Bronx

1. Public Safety Answering Center II
SKIDMORE, OWINGS & MERRILL (SOM), 2016 – 350 MARCONI STREET

A blast-proof, primarily windowless cube wrapped in serrated aluminum, PSAC II is an impenetrable but highly visible building that gives expression to the city's 911 services.

2. Via Verde
GRIMSHAW AND DATTNER ARCHITECTS, 2012 – 700 BROOK AVENUE

A stunning example of what affordable housing can be, this 222-unit project steps up from a courtyard amphitheater to a 20-story tower, providing residents spots for rooftop farming.

Brooklyn

3. 325 Kent
SHOP ARCHITECTS, 2017

The first piece completed in Two Trees's huge mixed-use development on the former Domino Sugar site is a copper-and-zinc-clad apartment building with a large portal facing Manhattan.

4. Brooklyn Botanic Garden Visitor Center

WEISS/MANFREDI, 2012 – 990 WASHINGTON AVENUE

This flowing building splits into two to funnel people into BBG, just as it meanders along existing paths and lets the landscape grow on top of it to merge building and garden.

5. LeFrak Center at Lakeside

TOD WILLIAMS BILLIE TSIEN ARCHITECTS, 2013 – 171 EAST DRIVE

This building embeds itself into Olmsted and Vaux's Prospect Park and provides two skating rinks, one open and the other covered by a bright blue plane carved with curling lines and dots of light.

6. Naval Cemetery Landscape

NELSON BYRD WOLTZ & MARVEL ARCHITECTS, 2016 –
63 WILLIAMSBURG STREET WEST

The former unmarked burial ground is open to the public as a wildflower meadow and sacred grove circled by a wooden boardwalk and accessed through a pavilion gateway.

7. Weeksville Heritage Center

CAPLES JEFFERSON ARCHITECTS, 2014 – 158 BUFFALO AVENUE

A low-slung, L-shaped building covered in wood and slate works with the landscape to embrace three mid-nineteenth-century houses from Weeksville, one of America's first free black communities.

Manhattan

8. 53W53

ATELIERS JEAN NOUVEL, 2019 – 53 WEST 53RD STREET

Although the city forced The Museum of Modern Art's second tower on its midtown block to trim 200 feet (61 m), down to 1,050 feet (320 m), the asymmetrically tapered form and expressed bracing make it a Midtown standout.

9. 121E22

OFFICE FOR METROPOLITAN ARCHITECTURE (OMA), 2018 – 121 EAST 22ND STREET

The Toll Brothers go avant-garde with a design by OMA's Shohei Shigematsu that features a prismatic volume on Lexington and 23rd Street and an undulating façade on 22nd Street.

10. 152 Elizabeth Street

TADAO ANDO ARCHITECT & ASSOCIATES, 2018

Developer Sumaida + Khurana's first project is also Tadao Ando's first building in NYC, with a concrete plinth that wraps up the sides and full-height glass walls at the corner.

11. Apple Fifth Avenue

FOSTER + PARTNERS, 2018 – 767 FIFTH AVENUE

Version 3.0 of Apple's subterranean NYC flagship follows two iterations by Bohlin Cywinski Jackson and features circular skylights dotting the plaza still punctuated by its signature glass cube.

12. Carmel Place

NARCHITECTS, 2016 – 335 EAST 27TH STREET

Prefab and micro-living converge in this competition-winning project with 55 residential units covered in four shades of brick on a narrow site in Kips Bay.

13. The Hills at Governors Island Park

WEST 8, 2016

The team led by West 8 piled debris from Governors Island's old buildings to create four hills at the south end of the otherwise flat island and give visitors an amazing overlook of New York Harbor.

14. The New School University Center
SKIDMORE, OWINGS & MERRILL (SOM), 2014 – 63 FIFTH AVENUE

The new vertical campus for The New School houses a dorm, library, auditorium, studios, and other educational spaces behind a copper-shingled façade cut up by a network of glass-enclosed stairs.

15. Sugar Hill Development
ADJAYE ASSOCIATES, 2015 – 898 ST. NICHOLAS AVENUE

A dark mass with 124 units of affordable housing is full of large and small gestures: a shifted volume at the ninth floor; serrated profiles on two façades; and rose patterns in the precast concrete.

16. Times Square Reconstruction
SNØHETTA, 2016

The city closed sections of Broadway to cars in 2009, but it took seven years to make it permanent, with dark paving, granite benches, and minimal lighting keeping the focus on the intersection's signage.

Queens

17. Kew Gardens Hills Library
WORKAC, 2017 – 72-33 VLEIGH PLACE, FLUSHING

The renovation and expansion of a small 1960s branch of Queens Library features a concrete façade lifted at its corner to reveal the interior, and a dip by the entry that showcases the green roof.

18. TWA Hotel
LUBRANO CIAVARRA ARCHITECTS & BEYER BLINDER BELLE, 2019 –
TERMINAL 5, JFK AIRPORT

Closed since October 2001, Eero Saarinen's iconic TWA Flight Center from 1962 is set to open as the lobby of a 505-room hotel in two curved wings flanking the birdlike symbol of aviation.

Staten Island

19. New York Public Library Stapleton Branch

ANDREW BERMAN ARCHITECT, 2013 – 132 CANAL STREET

The renovation and expansion of an early twentieth-century Carrère & Hastings public library is all glass and metal outside, but a wood structure warms an interior bathed in natural light.

20. Richmond County Supreme Court

ENNEAD ARCHITECTS, 2015 – 26 CENTRAL AVENUE

Sitting atop a hill southwest of two Carrère & Hastings landmarks, this large building covered in glass, precast concrete, and copper fronts the Memorial Green where a former burial ground was located.

Acknowledgments

Leading architectural walking tours was the last thing on my mind when this out-of-work architect wrote *Guide to Contemporary New York City Architecture* in the midst of the recession about ten years ago. So thanks first to the institutions that have hosted my tours over the years and made them a regular companion to the writing about architecture that has since become my day job. These include Van Alen Institute and its short-lived (and much missed) Van Alen Books, Open House New York, and the Scarsdale Adult School, but most of all the 92nd Street Y, which has been a stable supporter of my walking tours since 2012, first through its 92YTribeca location and, after it closed, its main location on East 92nd Street. Thanks in particular to Alicia Harris-Fernandez at 92Y and Jill Serling at SAS. Thanks also to the visiting architects, many from Sweden, who have commissioned me for tours and pushed me to explore the city beyond my regular routes.

NYC Walks: Guide to New Architecture has been greatly improved by a number of professional contributions. Thanks to Holly La Due at Prestel for believing in the project and seeing it through from start to finish. I'm grateful to Pavel Bendov for contributing photos from his book *New Architecture New York*, also from Prestel, and taking some great new ones for this book. Thanks to Peter Ahlberg for giving the tours a useful and beautiful layout, and for working with me on producing the maps. John Son's astute copyediting and fact-checking made me come across as a much more articulate guide. And thanks to Emma Kennedy and Ayesha Wadhawan at Prestel for all their help throughout the project.

Lastly, thanks to the family and friends who have accompanied me on the many scouting trips that eventually coalesced into walking tours—and the book you hold in your hands.

Index

© Prestel Verlag, Munich · London · New York 2019
A member of Verlagsgruppe Random House GmbH
Neumarkter Strasse 28 · 81673 Munich

Prestel Publishing Ltd.
14-17 Wells Street
London W1T 3PD

Prestel Publishing
900 Broadway, Suite 603
New York, NY 10003

Library of Congress Cataloging-in-Publication Data

Names: Hill, John, 1973- author.
Title: NYC walks : guide to new architecture / by John Hill.
Other titles: New York City walks : guide to new architecture
Description: Munich ; New York : Prestel, 2019.
Identifiers: LCCN 2018026678 | ISBN 9783791384900 (pbk.)
Subjects: LCSH: Architecture--New York (State)--New York--History--21st
  century--Tours. | Walking--New York (State)--New York--Tours. | New York
  (N.Y.)--Buildings, structures, etc.--Tours. | New York (N.Y.)--Tours.
Classification: LCC NA735.N5 H56 2019 | DDC 720.9747/0905--dc23
LC record available at https://lccn.loc.gov/2018026678

A CIP catalogue record for this book is available from the British Library.

Editorial direction: Holly La Due
Book design + layout: AHL&CO
Map design: Peter Ahlberg, Alexandra Veryovka, and John Hill
Production: Anjali Pala
Copyediting: John Son
Proofreading: Susan Richmond

Verlagsgruppe Random House FSC® N001967

Printed in China

ISBN: 978-3-7913-8490-0

www.prestel.com